ORAL TRADITION AS A LIVING TRADITION IN GREEK POETICS,

By Tony Malliaras, 2016.

Below: Aeneas fleeing from the flames of Troy, reproduced from "The History of the World" possessed by Schliemann as a child. *Schliemann of Troy*, by Emil Ludwig, New York: G.P. Putnam's Sons, 1930: 107.

Cover: *Hermes: Messenger of the Gods*, circa 480 BCE. Copyright University of Indiana Art Museum, 2018. All Rights Reserved. Front Page: Fresco from Pylos showing a lyre player circa 1700-1200 BCE. Perhaps a distant fore-runner of Homer. In Vol. II, The Frescoes of Mabel L. Lang, *The Palace of Nestor at Pylos in Western Messenia* copyright © 1969 by Princeton University Press. All Rights Reserved.

This paper was written during the winter of 2016 whilst completing the Honors in Musicology equivalent degree program at the University of Melbourne.

Oral Traditions as a Living Tradition in Greek Poetics by Tony Malliaras is copyrighted, 2018. All Rights Reserved.

Contents
1. Introduction.   8
2. Introduction II   11
3. Homer's *Iliad* and *Odyssey* in Cinema: *Ulysses* 1954 and *Troy* 2004 and the $1 Million-dollar *Euphronios* Crater 6th century BCE.
4. Oral Tradition and Ancient Poetic Tradition.
5. What influenced Greek Tradition?   15
6. Schliemann's Bible: The *Iliad* and *Odyssey* and *Pausania's Guide to Greece*.   18
7. Historical Incidents in the Ancient Record of the Hittites as Indicators for *Homer's Troy*.   20
8. Homer's Poetics as Eternal Values vs Homer as Historian.   25
9. Homer and the portrait of the powerful network of independent Mycenaean Greek kingdoms 1700 – 1150 BCE.   27
10. Homer's mastery of the Greek language and use of the epithet to convey meaning and vision.   35
11. Homer as the last of the great poet bards and transmitter of the Mycenaean Greek Bronze Age Palaces 1700 – 1150 BCE.   35
12. Homer and Musical Instruments in Performance and Practice.
13. Mycenaean Greek Kingdoms and the Hittite Empire and Vassal Confederacy 1500- 1150 BCE.   36
14. Homer as a Singer of Tales, as Performer, as Composer, as a Poet.   38
15. Homer as a Living Tradition of an Ancient Greek Tradition 2200 – 1150 BCE.   40
16. Homer and Fixed Formulas and System of Systems of Formulas in Orality   44
17. Homer and the Dactylic Hexameter and the modern Yugoslav bards: A Comparison in Orality.   46
18. Homer and Spatial Mnemonics in Performance and Theater.   47
19. Homeric Formula: How does it operate? What structure does it have?   48
20. Traditional formulaic texture underlies Homeric Formulas.   49
21. Homer's Mastery of expanding and contracting his Characters and use

of ornamentation. 49
22. Homer's improvisational methods vs Yugoslav bards in 1935 in comparison.
23. Homer's use of the Noun Verb and Noun Epithet Phrase Formula. 49
24. Homer's Storehouse of Similes. 51
25. Homer and the Heroic Character via the Operative Recurrent Ornamental Epithets.
26. Homer and the Greek language as the bearer of meaning in Performance. 51
27. Homer and the *Aulos* wind instrument and the *Phorminx* stringed instrument in performance in Mycenaean Courts 1700-1150 BCE. 57
28. Homer and Sailor's Yarns of Gilgamesh, King of Uruk 2700-2600 BCE.
29. Aristotle as champion of Homer vs Homer's detractors. 67
30. Homer's Training in the School of Talented Poets 800- 700 BCE. 73
31. Homer's Stock Phrases. 74
32. Homeric Formulae and Homeric Meter: Length and Thrift of Word Usage. 82

33. Homer's use of juxtaposition in the *Iliad* and *Odyssey*. 92
34. Conclusion. 92

Introduction

I shall always remember my second trip to Greece, in July 1986. My family touched down in Athens, Greece, disembarking from *Olympic Airways* and driving to a relative who lived next to the Parthenon. The incessant sound of the jack hammer breaking concrete filled my ears, as our taxi stopped at our destination. The Parthenon, looming overhead, made an immediate impression on me. I saw my father George, go off and talk to some builders taking a break. My father came back and told us that restoration work on the Parthenon had entered its second decade. Adding the original Parthenon took only 8 years to complete. I asked my father what problems did the architects and builders involved on restoration work on the Parthenon still have, after 20 years? "They can't locate the original plans of the master builder, Ictinus, who probably burned his plans". I asked my father who Ictinus was and why his plans are so important in relation to the Parthenon? My father answered, "Ictinus was a master of proportion and the curve. Ictinus alone knew where all the pieces of the Parthenon fit correctly". The Athenian statesman Pericles directed the architects Ictinus and Callicrates under the supervision of the sculptor Phidias to build the Parthenon in 447 – 438 BCE.[1] My father asked me if I thought the columns supporting the Parthenon were straight? I looked at the columns from a distance of 100 meters and said that they appear straight. "The columns are curved," he replied. It is interesting to note that none of the straight lines seen in the Parthenon are geometrically straight. Such concepts of making architecture appear to look correct are known as counter-perspective.[2] My father said, "The Ancient Greeks sought beauty not only in their temples, but in their poetry and language". I asked my father for only one example of such beauty in orality in the context of Greek tradition? "*Homiros* [Homer]", he replied, handing me a copy of Homer's *Iliad* and *Odyssey* in Greek. This paper is for my father George Malliaras, the Achaean Greek exemplar and my mother Hrysanthi, a true, Penelope.

---

[1] "Parthenon", in Last modified June 19, 2016, URL: www.britannica.com/topic/Parthenon.
[2] "Counter-perspective in the Parthenon Temple", Last modified June 19, 2016. in URL: www.math.nus.edu.sg/aslaksen/projects/perspective/parthenon.htm.

Undergraduates at University who wish to explore the terminology of this thesis can turn to Nicholas Richardson's, *The Iliad: A Commentary. Volume VI: Books 21-24*, 1993. 363-387. A. Gehring, *Index Homericus*, Hildesheim: G. Olms, 1970. William Bishop Owen and Edgar Johnson Goodspeed's *Homeric Vocabularies: Greek and English Word Lists for the Study of Homer*, Oklahoma City: Oklahoma Press, 1969. John Richard Cunliffe's *Homeric Lexicon*, Oklahoma City: University of Oklahoma Press, 2012. And J. R. Major, *Guide to the Reading of Greek Tragedians: The Greek Drama, Greek Metres and Canons of Criticism*, London: Longman, Brown, Green & Longmans, 1844.

Homer's poetry was sung by bards, often to the accompaniment of a lyre. It is written in dactylic hexameter, a metrical pattern in which the line is broken up into six feet, each foot consisting of a long syllable followed by two short syllables. In any foot the two short syllables may be replaced by a second- long syllable. Every single line of Greek in Homer's work follows this meter. Meeting these tight metrical constraints, line-opening or line-closing epithets that meet the metrical standards, such as "godlike Achilles" or "much-enduring Odysseus," permeate the Homeric epics. These stock phrases make memorization as well as on-the-spot composition much easier for the bard.

Exercises in *Homer's dactylic hexameter* can be practised via a combination of reading verse and music performance. By playing a lyre and moving the bow back and forth or back turning and back stretched. A Fiddler-man Master Violin Outfit with Fret board and progressing through lessons and crossing the bridge from reading music sheets to transposing and composing, students can learn to memorize passages from Homer's *Iliad & Odyssey*. Listening to Anthony Heald's narration of Homer in *Homer Box Set: Iliad & Odyssey Audio book* is also useful. Metrical rules should be kept in mind. Robert Fagles describes Homer's Greek as: the creation of epic verse using the hexameter or six metrical units, which may, be either dactyls a long plus two shorts or spondees or two longs in the first four places but must be dactyl and spondee in that order in the last two rarely spondee and spondee, never spondee followed by dactyl.[3] Importantly, the syllables are long and short, the meter is based on pronunciation time, not, as in the

---

[3] Robert Fagles, translator. *Homer: The Iliad*, New York: Penguin Books, 1990: 12.

English language, on stress.[4] Exercise 1: *Imitation*: Read and Memorize a passage from Book 1: The Rage of Achilles of Robert Fagle's translation of *Homer's Iliad & Odyssey*, New York: Penguin Books, 1990. Exercise 2: *Plot*: Book 2: The Great Gathering of Armies. Exercise 3: *Spectacle: Spatial*. Book 3: Helen Reviews the Champions. Exercise 4: *Tragedy*: Magnify and Reduce Themes. Book 4: The Truce Erupts into War. Exercise 5: *Character*: Magnify and Reduce Characters. Book 5: Diomedes Fights the Gods. Exercise 6: *Signs and Portends*: Book 6. Exercise 7: *Metaphor and Ornamentation*: Book 7. Exercise 8: *Language*: The old Greek principle of juxtaposition of longs and shorts. Book 8: The Tide of Battle Turns. Exercise 9: *Parallel and Dissimilar Lines*: Book 9: The Embassy to Achilles. Exercise 10: *Stock Phrases and Noun-Epithet Formulas*: Book 10: Marauding Through the Night. Exercise 11: *Epithets and Fixed Metrical Units*: Play Lyre with Bow back turning and back stretched faster. An Epithet is a characterizing word or phrase accompanying or occurring in place of the name of a person or thing. Book 11: Agamemnon's Day of Glory. Exercise 12: *Caesura* or a break in the flow of sound in a verse caused by the ending of a word within a foot. Book 12: The Trojans Storm the Rampart. Exercise 13: *Enjambment* or the running over of a sentence from one verse or couplet into another so that closely related words fall in different lines. Book 13: Battling for the Ships. Exercise 14: *Strophe* or a rhythmic system composed of two or more lines repeated as a unit; *especially*: such a unit recurring in a series of strophic units. Book 14. *Dactyl* a metrical foot consisting of one long and two short syllables or of one stressed and two unstressed syllables. Book 14: Hera Outflanks Zeus. Exercise 15: *Hexameter* a line of verse consisting of six metrical feet. Book 15: The Achaean Armies at Bay. Exercise 16: *Improvisation*. Book 16: Patroclus Fights and Dies. Exercise 17: *Genealogies of Gods and Men and Women*. Book 17: Meneleus' Finest Hour. Exercise 18: The Heroic Model: *Achilles and Odysseus*. Book: 18: The Shield of Achilles. Exercise 19: *Olympian Gods and the men and women on the battlefield at Troy*. Book 19: The Champion Arms for Battle. Exercise 20: *Bard or Poet as a nexus between the Gods and Men on the Battlefield of Troy*. Book 20: Olympian Gods in Arms. Exercise 21: *Mycenaean Magic and Religion*. Book 21: Achilles Fights the River. Exercise 22: *The Muses and access to divine knowledge*. Book: 22: The Death of Hector. Exercise 23: *Violence and Death*. Book 23: Funeral Games for Patroclus. Exercise 24: Homer. *Poet of Poets*. Book 24: Achilles and Priam.

---

[4] Fagles, *Homer: The Iliad*: 1990: 12.

Priority should be given to recording one's progress daily via a Sony HD Movie Camera. Over three years see how using Homer as a role model helps undergraduates and laymen to memorize the *Iliad and the Odyssey* and become musicians and poets.

Introduction II:

The main argument of this paper focusses on Oral Tradition as a Living Tradition in Greek Poetics. The exact nature and improvisational art of the Ancient Greek Poets and Bards may have been lost to us. However, an examination of the most authentic and ancient sources and modern scholarship sheds light on the world class poet known to history as Homer, who composed the celebrated Iliad and Odyssey which have thrilled audiences for more than 2700 years.

> To understand Homer and his great epics the *Iliad* and the *Odyssey*, composed around 700 BC. A look at the Mycenaean Kingdoms and the vast network of highly organized Greek kingdoms which existed 1600 – 1100 BCE is warranted. Bards who sang at the Courts of the Mycenaean Kings developed a highly organized improvisational singing which included what Aristotle called Homer's systems upon systems. Georg Danek and Stefan Hagel describes Homeric singing thus:
>
>> Epic performance was originally sung, in Ancient Greece (Demodokos!) as well as in many other traditions. The Greek *aoidoi*[5] sang to the accompaniment of the lyre (*phorminx*). The performance of Ancient Greek verse, as heard today, which involves the *ictus* that overrides the word accents is far removed from ancient pronunciation in several respects. Ancient Greek had a pitch accent, that is, the accent was expressed by means of pitch contour, not of stress. Extant settings of ancient music show that in traditional non-strophic poetry the melody followed the accentual contours. Thus, the melodies of early Greek hexameter poetry are not unlikely to have been governed by word accent and sentence intonation. There is statistical proof that end-accented words are avoided at caesura but favoured at metrical bridges. The melody of the 'typical' hexameter fell at the middle caesura as well as at the end of the verse. The 'typical' melodic contour consisted of a double, sometimes triple rise and fall. Less common verses have deviant melodic contours. E.g., in cases of strong enjambement, when the sentence lacks completion at verse end, we encounter a rising contour in the last third of the verse which lacks its completion by a melodic

---

[5] Aoidoi: Greek Bards who sang at the courts of Mycenaean Nobles in Encyclopedia Britannica https://www.britannica.com/art/aoidos. **Last Modified 24/8/2018.**

fall. Sentence and melodic trajectory are completed in the next verse.
These results give rise to a technique of Homeric performance which can be acquired. The performer must accommodate the accentual rises and falls of the individual words of each verse to the melodic contour which results from syntactical and metrical features. With some training, anyone who can read Homer can learn to improvise the melody to any given Homeric text. Individual accents produce smaller deviations from the overall melody (as in the extant musical documents). Each (major) accent may be realized by a rise to the accented syllable but must be followed by a melodic fall. In the case of circumflex syllables, the post-accentual fall may be realized on the second part of the accented syllable, resulting in a two-note 'melisma'.[6] The gravis accent forces the melody to rise without any downtrend up until the next accented syllable. Greek hexameter poetry is stichic.[7] Enjambement[8] should not by expressed by shortening or skipping the pause/instrumental interlude between the verses, but only by means of melody. On the other hand pauses within the verse are incompatible with Greek versification.[9]

---

[6] Melisma *the most poetic words can be given more emotive power by using melisma'* in URL: https://en.oxforddictionaries.com/definition/melisma. Last Modified 24/8/2018.

[7] Stichic of, relating to, or consisting of lines that are rhythmic units: arranged or divided by lines : serial in succession or recurrence. URL: https://www.merriam-webster.com/dictionary/stichic. Last Modified 24/8/2018.

[8] Enjambement (in verse) the continuation of a sentence without a pause beyond the end of a line, couplet, or stanza.in https://en.oxforddictionaries.com/definition/enjambement. Last Modified 24/8/2018.

[9] "Homeric Singing – An Approach to the Original Performance," Georg Danek and Stefan Hagel, University of Vienna, Last modified August 8, 2018. URL: https://www.oeaw.ac.at/kal/sh/index.htm.

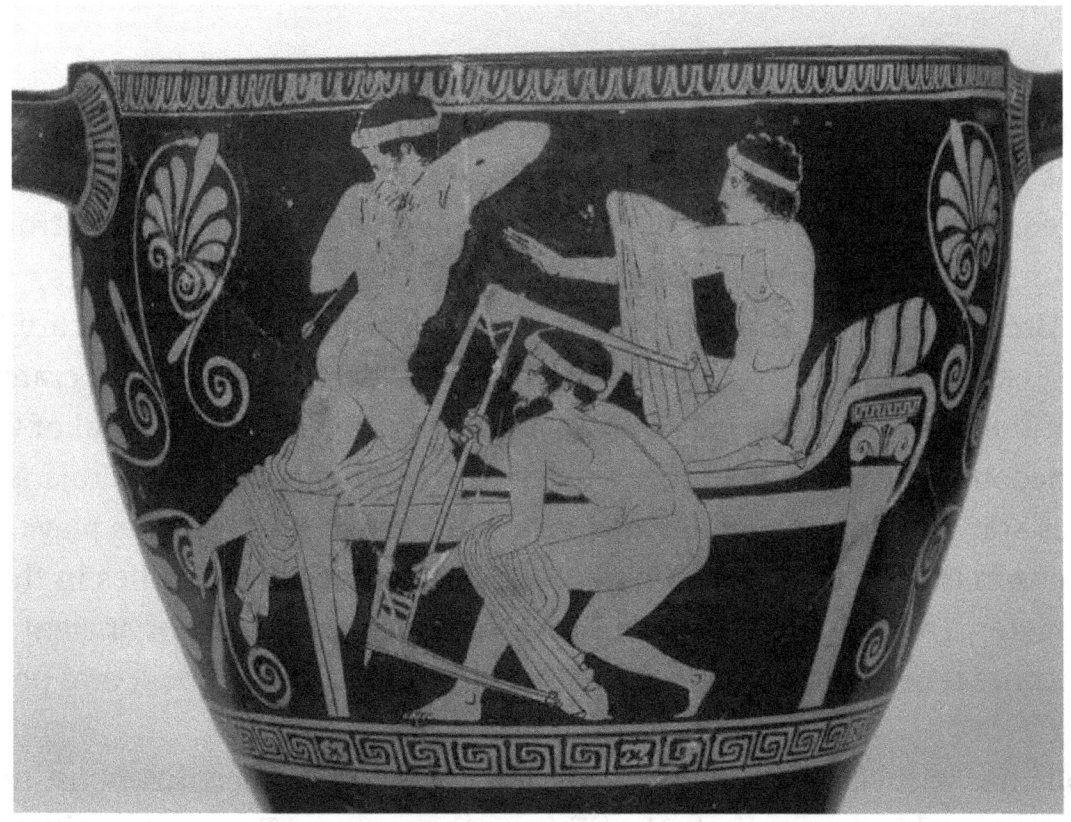

Death of the Suitors, Copyright Oxford University Press, 2018. All Rights Reserved.

The popularity of Homer's *Iliad* and *Odyssey* over 2700 years is depicted on famous vases to two epic movies. For example, on the NBC Today Show: Vase Unveiled, November 12, 1972, Curator Dietrich von Bothmer, of the Metropolitan Museum, New York, states, the *Euphronios* crater cost $1 million dollars,[10] the finest Greek vase there is, by two great Athenian artists in the 6th century BCE, the potter Euxitheos and the painter Euphronios.[11] He describes the large crater in the style of the late archaic period. The most moving subject, the removal of the body of Sarpedon while the twin brothers sleep in death flanked by two Trojans with Hermes standing behind. A truly memorable picture.[12] Kirk Douglas plays Odysseus in the popular move, *Ulysses* 1954.[13] Brad Pitt plays Achilles in the blockbuster, *Troy* 2004.[14] Karl Meyer provides a succinct outline of ancient Anatolia in the context of oral tradition and history, in connection to Greek oral poesy, stating:

Anatolia has witnessed a unique procession of peoples and civilizations. In this varied landscape one finds Neolithic settlement and Bronze Age cities, and, in a continuous chronology, the mingled artifacts of the Hittites, the Assyrians, the Phrygians, the Lydians, the Ionian Greeks, the Persians, the Armenians, the Hellenistic Greeks, the Romans, the Byzantines, the Arabs, the Seljuks, the Frankish Crusaders and the Ottoman Turks.[15]

Oral tradition has a rich history, which predates written poetic tradition. For example, ritual formulae in the Pyramid texts of King Wenis, is highly developed, and concepts of spirit, essence and power are prevalent.[16] Further, the 759 utterances[17] of the High Priest evoked power over the soul of the King, transforming him into a celestial being in the region known as the Imperishable Stars.[18] The oral composer relies on an ancient tradition and specialized training to

---

[10] Karl E. Meyer, *The Plundered Past: The Traffic in Art Treasures,* (London, Reader's Union, 1974): 302.
[11] Meyer, *The Plundered Past*: 87.
[12] Meyer, *The Plundered Past*: 307.
[13] *Ulysses*, Directed by Mario Camerini, 1954. DVD.
[14] *Troy*, Directed by Wolfgang Petersen, 2004. DVD.
[15] Karl Meyer, *The Plundered Past: The Traffic in Art Treasures*, (London, Trowbridge & Esher, 1974): 56.
[16] R. O. Faulkner, translator, *The Ancient Egyptian Pyramid Texts*, (Oxford: Oxford University Press, 1969): v-
[17] Faulkner, *The Ancient Egyptian Pyramid Texts*: 319.
[18] Faulkner, *The Ancient Egyptian Pyramid Texts*: 276.

convey power, through the spoken word. Steven Mithen argues that the late Ice Age artists, 23,000 BCE ... linked the social, spiritual, and natural worlds into a single continuum and that the environment was imbued with great potency.[19] Further, that all this art conveys complex, long forgotten ideas, a symbolic world of spirit animals and spirit humans, of forces benevolent and evil.[20]

What influenced Greek tradition? The Minoan Civilization 2000 – 1450 BCE divided into nine periods; with its palace at Knossos; boasted a high degree of civilization.[21] The Cretans were re-known mariners; their large ships transported gold, silver, obsidian, ivory, and ornaments from central Europe, the Aegean, and Southwest Asia.[22] An important feature of their religion centered on palaces, caves, and shrines where, apparently, people offered sacrifices to individuals who metamorphosed themselves into deities.[23] The Cretan Zeus and Earth Mother gods also existed in early tradition.[24] The Mycenaean used a form of script written in the Greek language, known as Linear B.[25] Eighty -nine characters make up Linear B, 48 of which can be traced back to Minoan writing, Linear A.[26]

---

[19] Brian M. Fagan, *People of the Earth: An Introduction to World Prehistory*, (Santa Barbara, Longman Press, 1998): 137.
[20] Fagan, *People of the Earth*: 137.
[21] Fagan, *People of the Earth*: 482-483.
[22] Fagan, *People of the Earth*: 483.
[23] Fagan, *People of the Earth*: 483.
[24] Fagan, *People of the Earth*: 484.
[25] Fagan, *People of the Earth*: 488.
[26] Fagan, *People of the Earth*: 488.

Hector, Andromache, and Astyanax, Copyright Oxford University Press, 2018. All Rights Reserved.

Polyphemos talks to his head ram. Copyright Oxford University Press, 2018. All Rights Reserved.

What inspired the wealthy merchant Heinrich Schliemann to excavate at Mycenae and Troy? Why did he have so much faith in Homer's *Iliad* and what did he use as a guide to help him find the site of Mycenae and Troy? Who validated Schliemann's finds? British Archaeologist Arthur Evans states that Heirich Schliemann was inspired by a picture of Anchises and Aeneas escaping from the flames of Troy, subsequently unearthing nine cities at Troy on the hill at Hissarlik, Turkey.[27] Schliemann's ability for acquiring new languages got him a job with Schroeder of Amsterdam as manager of their Russian branch.[28] He used his immense wealth from the indigo trade; California gold rush; and profits from the Crimean War to excavate at Mycenae and Troy.[29] Evans states, that Schliemann considered himself, an ancient Greek, addressing prayers to Zeus and Athene; and his literal belief in the records of Homer and practical use of *Pausania's Guide to Greece,* unearthed gold in Mycenae and Troy,[30] now housed in the Berlin Museum.[31]

---

[27] Emil Ludwig, *Schliemann of Troy: The Story of a Gold-seeker*, (London, Unwin Brothers Limited, 1931): 10.
[28] Ludwig, *Schliemann of Troy*: 10.
[29] Ludwig, *Schliemann of Troy*: 10.
[30] Ludwig, *Schliemann of Troy*: 12.
[31] Ludwig, *Schliemann of Troy*: 23.

What historical incidents influenced Homer's Troy? Who were the Trojans? What influence did Mycenaean Greeks have on Western Anatolia from Hittite records? From 2000 BCE the populations of Anatolia included three groups who spoke Indo-European languages.[32] The Hittites spoke Nesite and inhabited Central East Anatolia; the Palians who spoke Palai in the North- West Anatolia; and the Luwians who spoke Luwian in the West – South- West Anatolia.[33] Did the Trojans speak Luwian? The discovery of a [Luwian] hieroglyphic seal in Troy is suggestive but far from conclusive that Luwian was spoken.[34] Hittite records mention the names of the Kings of Wilusa or Troy from 1380-1322 BCE, King Alaksandu [Priam], King Kukkunni and King Walmu.[35]

Hittite records also state that the threat to Hittite interest in the west was intensified by an alliance with Arzawan King Uhhaziti formed with the King of Ahhiyawa [Mycenaean Greece], now becoming increasingly involved in Western Anatolian affairs.[36] Emil Forrer first put forward the theory that Wilusa – (W)ilios is Troy, mentioned in Hittite texts.[37] Despite fierce resistance to this theory at first, scholars now favor that (W)ilios with Troy.[38] If valid, it would go a long way to confirming the view, that the Trojans of level VI, if not their predecessors, were Luwian speaking peoples.[39] More importantly, it would provide a stronger basis for arguing for the fundamental historicity of the tradition of a Trojan War.[40] Furthermore, is there any connection to the Troy of Homer's Iliad? Wilusa first appears in Hittite texts, in the form of Wilusiya, as the penultimate name in the list of twenty- two countries which formed the Assuwan confederacy.[41] Troy is more narrowly identified with the last name in the list as Taruisa [Troy].[42] Despite the striking makeup and

---

[32] Craig H. Melchart, *Luwians*, Boston, Brill Academic Publishers, 2003: 27.
[33] Melchart, *Luwians*,: 27.
[34] Melchart, *Luwians*,: 11.
[35] Melchart, *Luwians*,: 12.
[36] Melchart, *Luwians*,: 59.
[37] Melchart, *Luwians*,: 68.
[38] Melchart, *Luwians*,: 68.
[39] Melchart, *Luwians*,: 68.
[40] Melchart, *Luwians*,: 68.
[41] Melchart, *Luwians*,: 68.
[42] Melchart, *Luwians*,: 68.

geographical extension between the Assuwan confederacy's comparison to Homer's catalogue of Troy's allies in Book II of the *Iliad*, the comparison is only slight.[43]

In effect, all that can be said of the Trojan Catalogue in a historical Anatolian context is that it reflects, broadly, the kind of alliance of countries that was common in western Anatolia during the late Bronze Age, as depicted by the Assuwan confederacy.[44] A further possible historical reference to the site, or region, in which Homer's Iliad is set, is mentioned on a silver bowl of unknown origin, which records the conquest of Tarwiza by Tudhaliya.[45] The texts also mention that Hittite King Muwattalli 1295 – 1272 BCE[46], ceded Millawanda [Miletos] to satisfy Ahhiyawan [Mycenaean] ambitions in Anatolia.[47]

Is the Trojan War Myth or Reality? Who are the people of the Homer's Iliad? Did as Homer sings in the Iliad, Agamemnon, the Greek King, command a united massive Greek armada of 1,186 ships against Troy?[48] Contact between mainland Greece and Troy is attested even in the Middle Bronze Age, circa 1900 – 1600 BCE.[49] From Hittite sources we learn that Mycenaean involvement Anatolian affairs covered a period of 200 years circa 1425 to 1225 B.C.E.[50] Miletos became the most important base for Mycenaean activity in western Anatolia.[51]

Mycenaean pottery in various sub-levels of [Troy] level VI reflects contacts between Troy and the Mycenaean Greeks.[52] Perhaps Mycenaean aggression was due to a squabble over the use of the Hellespont by Greek merchant ships; with Troy preventing Greek ships sailing through the Hellespont to the Black Sea.[53] The more likely candidate for Homeric Troy is the final phase of

---

[43] Melchart, *Luwians*,: 69.
[44] Melchart, *Luwians*,: 69.
[45] Melchart, *Luwians*,: 69.
[46] Gary M. Beckman, Trevor R. Bryce, and Eric H. Cline, *The Ahhiyawa Texts*, Atlanta, Society of Biblical Literature Press, 2011: 7.
[47] Melchart, *Luwians*: 69.
[48] Trevor Bryce, *Kingdom of the Hittites*, (Oxford; New York; Oxford University Press, 2005): 358.
[49] Bryce, *Kingdom of the Hittites*: 364.
[50] Bryce, *Kingdom of the Hittites*: 362.
[51] Bryce, *Kingdom of the Hittites*: 362.
[52] Bryce, *Kingdom of the Hittites*: 364.
[53] Bryce, *Kingdom of the Hittites*: 365.

the sixth level of the city – Troy VI h.[54] This level, with its imposing towers and distinctive sloping walls accords much better with the Homeric description of Priam's Troy than does its successor level.[55] Tudhaliya I, or II 1400 –1350 B.C.E.[56] had a further cause of complaint.[57] Madduwatta [his vassal] had been all too eager to lead his forces against the king of Arzawa.[58] But he failed to take any action at all in support of the Hittite forces when his old enemy Attarssiya invaded Hittite territory with the prime object of capturing him and killing him.[59] The Hittite texts read:

Subsequently Attarssiya, the man from Ahhiya [Mycenaean Greece], came, and plotted to kill you, Madduwatta. But when my father of My Sun heard of this, he dispatched Kisnapili, troops and chariots to do battle with Attarssiya. And you, Madduwatta offered no resistance to Attarssiya, and fled before him.[60] Hattusili III the Hittite King reigned from 1267 – 1237 B.C.E.[61] His letter of complaint to the

Ahhiyawan [Mycenaean Greek] King about his apparent support of the rebellious activity of Piyamaradu on Hittite territory is both conciliatory and yet reveals the humiliation and vexation Hattusili feels in asking for help from someone he knows is supporting Piyamaradu against Hattusili.[62]

The Tawagalawa letter reads:
According to this rumour, during this time when he leaves behind his wife, children, and household in my Brother's land, your land is affording him protection. But he is continually raiding my land; whenever I have prevented him in that, he comes back into your territory. Are you now, my Brother, favourably disposed in this conduct? (If not), now, my Brother, write at least

---

[54] Bryce, *Kingdom of the Hittites*: 365.
[55] Bryce, *Kingdom of the Hittites*: 365.
[56] Gary M. Beckman, Trevor R. Bryce, and Eric H. Cline, *The Ahhiyawa Texts*, Atlanta, Society of Biblical Literature Press, 2011: 7.
[57] Bryce, *The Ahhiyawa Texts*: 133.
[58] Bryce, *The Ahhiyawa Texts*: 133.
[59] Bryce, *The Ahhiyawa Texts*: 133.
[60] Bryce, *The Ahhiyawa Texts*: 133.
[61] Gary M. Beckman, Trevor R. Bryce, and Eric H. Cline, *The Ahhiyawa Texts*, Atlanta, Society of Biblical Literature Press, 2011: 7.
[62] Bryce, *The Ahhiyawa Texts*: 292.

this to him: 'Rise up, go forth into the Land of Hatti. Your lord has settled this account with you! Otherwise, go into the land of the Ahhiyawa [Land of Mycenaean Greeks] and in whatever place I settle you, [you must remain there]. Rise up with your prisoners, your wives and children, and settle down in another place! So long as you are at enmity with the king of Hatti exercise your hostility from (some) other country! From my country, you shall not conduct hostilities!'[63]

Webster argues that there were three main kinds of poetry sung by balladists or minstrels performing as entertainers for Mycenaean kings and noblemen circa 1400 – 1100 B.C.E.[64] Cult songs, songs about the great kings of the past on anniversaries, and songs sung at banquets, which focused which dealt with the international present but laid strong emphasis on the local king.[65]

In the *Iliad*, Homeric society consisted of three different periods – the Mycenaean Age 1400 – 1100 B.C.E., the so- called Dark Age 1100 – 800 B.C.E., and the Iron Age, 700 B.C.E.[66] The story of the Trojan War is almost certainly a literary conflation, in which there was a gradual accumulation of traditions, inspired by a range of historical incidents.[67] There may have been one or more Dark Age poets to whom the bard's mantle should be assigned, or at least, should be shared.[68] A letter from a King of Ahhiyawa [Mycenaean Greek King] to a King of Hatti (probably Muwattalli II 1290-1250 BCE, sheds light on this period.[69] Discussion in this badly damaged letter is primarily concerned with the rightful ownership of a group of islands that had seemingly formed part of a dowry in a previous generation.[70]

---

[63] Bryce, *The Ahhiyawa Texts*: 292.
[64] Bryce, *The Ahhiyawa Texts*: 368.
[65] Bryce, *The Ahhiyawa Texts*: 368.
[66] Bryce, *The Ahhiyawa Texts*: 369.
[67] Bryce, *The Ahhiyawa Texts*: 371.
[68] Bryce, *The Ahhiyawa Texts*: 371.
[69] Bryce, *The Ahhiyawa Texts*: 7.
[70] Bryce, *The Ahhiyawa Texts:* 134.

The letter reads:

[Thus says ..., Great King, King of Ahhiyawa [Mycenaean Greek King] [Say to His Majesty, King of Hatti]: [...] which [...] hostility [occurred] therein. [... And this] occurred. Then the [...] of the dead [...]. In the previous year my brother wrote to me: ["...] As for your islands that [you ...] the Storm God gave them to me in subjugation." The King of Assuwa [...] Kagamuna, [his (?)] great grandfather, [...] married previously. Then Tudhaliya, [your great grandfather, defeated the King of Assuwa] and subjugated him. [The islands formerly indeed belonged to the King of Ahhiyawa, and] I have now written [to my brother] on account [of this. But] to [...] and the King of Ahhiyawa [...] But in the past [...] then [...] in the land [of Hatti (?) ...] against [...] these [...] to [...]. 135.

Scholars argue that the King of Kings in the *Iliad* is the real life, version of Agamemnon based at Mycenae on the Greek mainland, who may have led a confederation of Mycenaean kingdoms or states.[71] In effect, the Ahhiyawa or Mycenaean Greeks were an early version of the Delian League, or Thalassocracy of Minos, a maritime confederacy which was led by the power elite at Mycenae.[72] The Hittites knew of the political conglomeration known as Assuwa, which they indicate was a confederation of twenty- two smaller cities and states in northwest Anatolia during 1425 BCE.[73] Based on twenty- five texts found at the archives of the Hittite capital city of Hattusa, Emil Forrer correctly linked the Ahhiyawa to the Mycenaeans of the Bronze Age Greek mainland, that is, the Achaeans.[74] He identified Lazpa in the Ahhiyawa texts as the island of Lesbos; Taruisa as the city of Troy; Attarissiya and Tawagalawa as the legendary Greek heroes Atreus and Eteokles.[75]

---

[71] Bryce, *The Ahhiyawa Texts*: 6.
[72] Bryce, *The Ahhiyawa Texts*: 6.
[73] Bryce, *The Ahhiyawa Texts*: 6.
[74] Bryce, *The Ahhiyawa Texts*: 1.
[75] Bryce, *The Ahhiyawa Texts*: 1.

Fight over Patroclus. Copyright Oxford University Press, 2018. All Rights Reserved.

In contrast, John Chadwick in the context of the historicity of the *Iliad* and *Odyssey* states, this is not to say that there are not tedious sections.[76] Archaeology has no means of telling us the names of the generals, nor even who the attacker's were.[77] John Chadwick argues that Homer's geography is faulty. For example, the so called Catalogue of Ships in Book 2 of the Iliad.[78] It lists nine towns, beginning with Pylos, which are subject to Nestor.[79] The Pylos tablets from 1230 BCE show nine areas of the Hither Province; but Pylos is not one of these nine, for it stands aloof from the tribute lists.[80]

Neither do any of the other names matches, though one Homeric name, Kyparisseeis, does appear to be a variant of a place name found on the tablets.[81] John Chadwick does clarify what Homer is. For example, he states, it is important to remember that Homer was a poet, not an historian.[82] Poetry is concerned with unchanging, eternal values; history with facts and events.[83] One suspicion is that Homer does not know in detail the geography of western Greece is evident.[84] For example, when he describes the location of Odysseus' home Ithaca, his geography is faulty.[85]

John Chadwick argues that Homer was an Ionian Greek who had probably never even sailed across the Aegean, let alone round the west coast of Greece.[86] What does concern us is the human values, the emotions and attitudes of the poet's characters; for these are constants of human nature, as important today as at any time in the past.[87] Worst of all, we do not know where he came from, despite seven cities claim to be his birthplace proves that the Greeks had no reliable

---

[76] John Chadwick, *The Mycenaean World*, Cambridge, Cambridge University Press, 1991: 182.
[77] Chadwick, *The Mycenaean World:* 185.
[78] Chadwick, *The Mycenaean World*: 185.
[79] Chadwick, *The Mycenaean World*: 185.
[80] Chadwick, *The Mycenaean World*: 185.
[81] Chadwick, *The Mycenaean World*: 186.
[82] Chadwick, *The Mycenaean World*: 186.
[83] Chadwick, *The Mycenaean World*: 186.
[84] Chadwick, *The Mycenaean World*: 186.
[85] Chadwick, *The Mycenaean World*: 186.
[86] Chadwick, *The Mycenaean World*: 186.
[87] Chadwick, *The Mycenaean World*: 186.

information.[88]

Maron gives the sack of potent wine to Odysseus. Copyright Oxford University Press, 2018. All Rights Reserved.

---

[88] Chadwick, *The Mycenaean World*: 183.

The Euphronius Crater, Metropolitan Museum, New York, United States of America. Copyright The MET, 2018. All Rights Reserved.

Homer's unusual name has led to speculation that he was not perhaps a Greek speaker, but introduced poetry to the Greeks.[89] Chadwick refutes, such a theory, as incompatible with the evidence of a long Greek oral tradition; Homer's predecessors undoubtedly spoke Greek.[90]

But it is evident that Homer inherited much of his technique from his unknown predecessors; he may equally have inherited much of the story.[91] This may explain how tradition has been handed down from one singer to the next, which binds Homer to the Mycenaean age.[92]

Is the Trojan War a historical event? Is the fresco from Pylos showing a lyre-player sitting on a rock, a distant fore-runner of Homer 1250 -700 B.C.E.? John Chadwick argues that of the nine cities on top of one another, Troy VIIA, seems to have been destroyed by enemy action around 1250 BCE.[93] Those who wish to save Homer's reputation can claim it as confirmation of the Trojan War.[94] John Chadwick argues that each poem shows evidence of a monumental structure, which implies a single architect.[95] The poems show a great deal of evidence of formulaic composition, but his work is generally at a far higher level.[96] Homer was not only a clever storyteller, but one of the world's great poets.[97] Why? Because he took the oral tradition and transformed it into superb poetry.[98]

---

[89] Chadwick, *The Mycenaean World*: 183.
[90] Chadwick, *The Mycenaean World*: 183.
[91] Chadwick, *The Mycenaean World*: 182.
[92] Chadwick, *The Mycenaean World*: 182.
[93] Chadwick, *The Mycenaean World*: 185.
[94] Chadwick, *The Mycenaean World*: 185.
[95] Chadwick, *The Mycenaean World*: 184.
[96] Chadwick, *The Mycenaean World*: 182.
[97] Chadwick, *The Mycenaean World*: 182.
[98] Chadwick, *The Mycenaean World*: 182.

Odysseus and Kalypso. Copyright Oxford University Press, 2018. All Rights Reserved.

Around 700 BCE a poet whose name was known later as *Homeros*, meaning hostage put together two large epic poems.[99] The *Iliad*, named after *Ilium*, the alternative name of Troy describes a short but vital period in the tenth year of the siege of that city by a Greek expeditionary force.[100]

The *Odyssey* is the story of the homecoming of Odysseus from the Trojan War.[101] Both poems are set in the same period, but are greatly removed from the date of their composition.[102] The Achaeans, as the Greeks were known in the Mycenaean Age.[103] In the 800 BCE Greece was a disorganized collection of petty states, still living at a contemporary low level of civilization; houses were mainly of wood and mud brick; precious materials were very scarce; the arts of painting and sculpture were primitive.[104]

Homer describes a Greece made up of a network of well- organized kingdoms capable of joint military action; its kings live in luxurious stone- built palaces, adorned with gold, ivory and other precious materials.[105] Homer's epics are a living link to the Mycenaean Age, to the 1200's or more likely 1300 BCE.[106] John Chadwick argues that there are more than a few elements in the Homeric poems which go back not to the end of the Mycenaean period but an earlier phase.[107] For example, one character in the *Iliad* has the great body shield described as 'like a tower', yet these seem to have gone out of use a couple of centuries earlier.[108] Another example is an exact description in Homer of a helmet covered in plates cut from boars' tusks; such an object was known in the early Mycenaean period 1600 BCE. but seems to have gone out of fashion by 1300 BCE.[109]

---

[99] Chadwick, *The Mycenaean World*: 180.
[100] Chadwick, *The Mycenaean World*: 180.
[101] Chadwick, *The Mycenaean World*: 180.
[102] Chadwick, *The Mycenaean World*: 180.
[103] Chadwick, *The Mycenaean World*: 180.
[104] Chadwick, *The Mycenaean World*: 180.
[105] Chadwick, *The Mycenaean World*: 180.
[106] Chadwick, *The Mycenaean World*: 180.
[107] Chadwick, *The Mycenaean World*: 183.
[108] Chadwick, *The Mycenaean World*: 183.
[109] Chadwick, *The Mycenaean World*: 183.

For example, striking formulas used to name a hero is to call him 'the holy might of Alkinoos' but he does not have to be particularly pious to deserve this appellation, and the word which to the later Greeks meant 'holy' may have started by meaning little more than 'powerful'.[110] Significantly, this same phrase without the proper name occurs also in the Vedic hymns; the Greek hieron menos is exactly paralleled by Vedic ishiram manas, not just in sense, 'mighty power', but these are in origin the very same two words.[111] John Chadwick believes that it seems probable that both languages have here preserved a very ancient expression.[112] The process of oral composition leaves characteristic traces on the poem.[113] For example, Homer, as a creative singer, creates new poems as he recites.[114]

Through a long process of imitation and improvisation, he has developed the ability to memorize group of lines, single lines, half lines and even smaller units suitable for all the normal situations.[115] There are numerous formulas for speech. For example, 'Thus indeed he spoke and addressed him with words that went flying'.[116] Hero epithets such as Akhilleus is 'fleet of foot', Odysseus 'much devising', Agamemnon 'king of men'.[117] The Greek language not only a rich vocabulary, it is also an inflected language, with different patterns of scansion in different cases so that the epithet has to change too.[118]

Ian Morris and Barry Powell convincingly argue from archaeological finds at Mycenae, Pylos and Tiryns that put Homer's epic poems to the Greek Bronze Age and a plausible link for the techniques of epic oral composition to the Bronze Age palaces, demonstrating epic song at least from an early period 1700 BCE to

---

[110] Chadwick, *The Mycenaean World*: 183.
[111] Chadwick, *The Mycenaean World*: 183.
[112] Chadwick, *The Mycenaean World*: 183.
[113] Chadwick, *The Mycenaean World*: 181.
[114] Chadwick, *The Mycenaean World*: 181.
[115] Chadwick, *The Mycenaean World*: 181.
[116] Chadwick, *The Mycenaean World*: 181.
[117] Chadwick, *The Mycenaean World*: 181.
[118] Chadwick, *The Mycenaean World*: 181.

Homer's day 700 BCE.[119] For example, the fresco of the lyre player at the Palace of Nestor is indicative of an oral poet in performance at a Mycenaean Court.[120]

More importantly, Homer preserves a memory of Bronze Age literacy in the famous Bellerophon episode and introduces it as yet another example of epic distance.[121] Morris and Powell argue that, the most significant element in the story, reflecting eastern writing practices with the Bronze Age is the Uluburun diptych tablet.[122]

Who are the people of Homer's *Iliad* and *Odyssey*? Is there are historical basis to the Trojan War?

Since Tudhaliya II's 1360 – 1344 B.C.E.[123] defeat of the Assuwan confederacy, the situation in the west had remained unstable, primarily as a result of the enterprises of a man named Madduwatta.[124] Having in some way made a mortal enemy of Arttarsiya, the man of Ahhiyawa that is, a Mycenaean Greek, Madduwatta fled to Hattusa, where he sought asylum in Tudhaliya II's court.[125] Muwatalli II 1295 – 1272 B.C.E.[126] had to deal with yet another renegade vassal, in the west, Piyamaradu, who may have taken control of the loyal vassalage of Wilusa.[127]

With the help of his vassals in Mira and the Seha River Land, Muwattali expelled Piyamaradu, who probably found refuge with the Ahhiyawans [Mycenaean Greeks], who were always ready to support anti-Hittite efforts in the region.[128] Western Anatolia is the logical genesis where the political structures first began to disintegrate in the struggle between the Hittite capital of Hatti, and the Ahhiyawans [Mycenaean Greeks].[129] Murli II or Urhi-Teshub 1272 – 1267

---

[119] Ian Morris, Barry B. Powell, Ed. *A New Companion to Homer,* (New York, E.J. Brill, 1997): 531. (See Fresco of a Lyre Player at Nestor's Palace).
[120] Morris & Powell, *A New Companion to Homer*: 531.
[121] Morris & Powell, *A New Companion to Homer*: 531.
[122] Morris & Powell, *A New Companion to Homer*: 532.
[123] Bryce, *The Ahhiyawa Texts*: 7.
[124] Billie Jean King, *The Hittites and their World*, Atlanta, Society of Biblical Literature, 2007: 44.
[125] King, *The Hittites and their World*: 44.
[126] Bryce, *The Ahhiyawa Texts*: 7.
[127] King, *The Hittites and their World*: 53.
[128] King, *The Hittites and their World*: 53.
[129] King, *The Hittites and their World*: 77.

B.C.E.[130] might have unsuccessfully sought the support of the king of Ahhiyawa [Mycenaen Greek King] before turning to Babylon.[131] Hattusili III 1267 – 1237 B.C.E.[132] wrote a long letter to the king of Ahhiyawa [Mycenaean Greeks], the Tawagalawa letter.[133] The main concern of which was the insurrectionist Piyamaradu, who had been harassing Hatti's western allies since Muwatalli's reign. Tawagalawa is the brother of the unknown Mycenaean Greek King.[134] Tudhaliya IV 1237 – 1209 B.C.E.[135] achieved an alliance against further aggression from the Mycenaean Greeks.[136] Tudhaliya IV also imposed a trade embargo against Assyria that forbade Shaushgamura of Amurru to allow ships from Ahhiyawa [Mycenaean Greece] to trade with Assyria via his ports.[137] Egyptian records from the reigns of Menerptah and Ramesses III describe battles with ship borne enemies whose unholy alliance included at various times, the Sherden, Ekwesh, Lukka, Teresh, Peleset, Tjeker, Shekelesh, Denyen, and Weshesh. The Ekwesh, connected with the Ahhiyawans [Mycenaean Greeks].[138]

---

[130] Bryce, *The Ahhiyawa Texts*: 7.
[131] King, *The Hittites and their World*: 60.
[132] Bryce, *The Ahhiyawa Texts*: 7.
[133] King, *The Hittites and their World*: 63-64.
[134] King, *The Hittites and their World*: 63-64.
[135] Bryce, *The Ahhiyawa Texts*: 7.
[136] King, *The Hittites and their World*: 67.
[137] King, *The Hittites and their World*: 68.
[138] King, *The Hittites and their World*: 77.

Nestor. Copyright Oxford University Press, 2018. All Rights Reserved.

What historical incidents inspired Homer's *Iliad* & *Odyssey*?

Homer, as a singer of tales, was also a performer, composer and poet at the same time.[139] The main difficulty for scholars who are against the oral tradition lies in the fact that the man singing an epic song is not a mere carrier of the tradition but a creative artist making the tradition.[140] The quarrel about the errors and inconsistencies in the Homeric poems, inherited from the seventeenth century, has continued steadily until our own times.[141]

Are there any Mycenaean relics in the *Iliad*?

Objects described in the Iliad point to the Mycenaean Greek era 1600 – 1150 BCE. For example, the boar's tusk helmet in the Tenth Book of the Iliad, worn by Greek warriors.[142] Martin Nilsson argues that such an object from the [Mycenaean Age 1600 – 1500 BCE] survived in the epic tradition.[143] The Ionic Greek version of Homer's epic which contains elements of Aeolic, which was spoken in the north of Greece; Arcadian in the south of Greece, is reflective of Mycenaean civilization and historical incidents in relation to the siege of Troy.[144] What was life like in Mycenaean Greece like and its influence on the Homeric Epics? Mycenae 1600 – 1100 BCE had no natural wealth, no gold or silver mines, or any exploitable commodity.[145] Yet the craftsmanship of her products implied intense specialization, and this in turn an economic system in which the means of life were available to specialized workers.[146] Pottery styles show the entry of proto- Greeks, entering Greece about 2000 BCE or earlier.[147] The Greek language is known from documents

---

[139] Albert B. Lord, *The Singer of Tales*, (Cambridge, Harvard University Press, 2000): 13.
[140] Lord, *The Singer of Tales*: 13.
[141] Lord, *The Singer of Tales*: 10.
[142] Denys L. Page, *History and the Homeric Iliad,* (Berkeley, University of California Press, 1966): 218.
[143] Page, *History and the Homeric Iliad*: 218-219.
[144] Page, *History and the Homeric Iliad*: 220-221.
[145] John Chadwick, *The Decipherment of Linear B*, (Cambridge, Cambridge University Press, 1958): 7.
[146] Chadwick, *The Mycenaean World*: xii.
[147] Chadwick, *The Mycenaean World*: xii.

written in Greece from 1400 BCE[148] but did not exist before 2200 BCE.[149] The 3,000 Linear B tablets at Knossos and 1,200 at Pylos; constitute unimpeachable information about the earliest Greek civilization.[150] If the Mycenaeans did not consider it necessary to preserve their history or diplomatic correspondence, at least they did leave a record of the administration of the kingdoms and the operation of some parts of their economy.[151] Interestingly, John Chadwick points to the oldest elements of Homer's epics; the god Zeus and the god Poseidon; stating that the ancestors of the Greeks brought these deities to Greece and that they are of Indo-European origin, from over 4000 years old in the context of tradition.[152]

---

[148] Chadwick, *The Mycenaean World*: 1.
[149] Chadwick, *The Mycenaean World*: 4.
[150] Chadwick, *The Mycenaean World*:15.
[151] Chadwick, *The Mycenaean World*: 15.
[152] Chadwick, *The Mycenaean World*: 86.

What role does philology, anthropology, have in relation to the Homeric Question?

The earliest scholarly anticipation of Homer's orality can be attributed to Flavius Josephus, born 37/38 CE, a Jewish priest, Pharisee.[153] Josephus states, [Homer's] poems were put together just as they were remembered distinctly from songs, and that through this process their many inconsistencies arose'.[154] Vasilii V. Radlov's fieldwork amongst the Kara Kirghiz singers of Turkic peoples of Central Asia circa 1885[155] found the following key elements in relation to orality. He states, 'every capable singer always improvises his songs for the presentation of the moment, so that he is never in the situation of reciting a song in precisely the same way twice. They do not that this improvisation constitutes an actual new composition'.[156] For instance: By virtue of extensive practice in recitation, he has in readiness entire sets of recitation parts … which he joins together in fitting ways during the course of his narration.

Such recitation parts consist of descriptions of certain occurrences and situations, like the birth of a hero, his coming of age, praise of weapons, preparation for battle, the sounds of battle, a hero's speech before battle, the description of individuals or of horses, the characteristics of renowned heroes, praise for a betrothed's beauty, portrayal of one's home, the law, a banquet, invitation to a feast, a hero's death, a funeral lament, description of a landscape, the onset of night and the break of day, and many others.[157]

Similarly, Friedrich Krauss's fieldwork of Yugoslav *guslars* in 1908 found that: The *guslar* invents nothing more of importance, since the fixed formulas, from which he neither can nor wishes to vary, are available to fulfill his needs through the centuries old bequest of the old tradition. To make a new song his own, that is, a song which is until that point composed of unfamiliar

---

[153] John Miles Foley, *The Theory of Oral Composition: History and Methodology*, Indianapolis, Indiana University Press, 1988: 2.
[154] Foley, *The Theory of Oral Composition*: 2.
[155] Foley, *The Theory of Oral Composition*: 10.
[156] Foley, *The Theory of Oral Composition*: 11.
[157] Foley, *The Theory of Oral Composition*: 11.

subject matter requires a practiced guslar who so thoroughly knows suitable [clichés] that he need only listen attentively in what order the [clichés] follow and whether in longer or shorter form, or in what connection they present themselves in the new set of circumstances.[158]

---

[158] Foley, *The Theory of Oral Composition*: 13.

What role does Homer have in captivating his audience via spatial devices or ability to make his audience envision a battle scene or dawn? Jenny Strauss Clay corroborates Milman Parry's thesis that Homer focused on verbal repetitions of formulaic expressions on the level of the individual hexameter lines, on type scenes in sequences of verses, and typical motifs and themes that form the larger building blocks of the narrative.[159] More importantly, she adds another cornerstone into the workings of Homer's mind by arguing that the opening invocation inaugurates that mediation as the poet asks the Muse to sing, the rage of Peleus' son, Achilles.[160] I agree with her argument that Homeric discourse is a special kind of discourse, a special language which provides a gateway to a world distinct from our own, inhabited by gods and heroes, distant but still comprehensible.[161] She demonstrates this by arguing that the Muses are the repository of this special kind of knowledge, of a vision. And the poet, in possession of this vision, conveys his audience to another place and another time, the Mycenaean world.[162] The heroic past cannot speak to us directly; it requires the mediation of the poet to be brought to life.[163] D. Rubin points to a powerful tool used by Homer or long line of poets from 1400 – 700 BCE:

[I]magery has many strengths as a way of increasing the memorability of an oral tradition. Imagery is one of our most powerful mnemonic aids. It is especially useful where the rapid retrieval of information is important, as it is in singing to a fixed rhythm, and where spatial layout and interacting components of a scene offer additional forms of organization. Imagery, by its very nature also seems well suited for the rapid transformations and actions ... that most oral traditions require ... In an oral tradition, imagery involves the transformation of a sequential verbal input into a spatial image and back to a sequential verbal output.[164]

---

[159] Jenny Strauss Clay, *Homer's Trojan Theater: Space, Vision, and Memory in the Iliad*, (Cambridge, Cambridge University Press, 2011): 14.
[160] Clay, *Homer's Trojan Theater: Space, Vision, and Memory in the Iliad*: 15.
[161] Clay, *Homer's Trojan Theater: Space, Vision, and Memory in the Iliad*: 15.
[162] Clay, *Homer's Trojan Theater: Space, Vision, and Memory in the Iliad*: 16-17.
[163] Clay, *Homer's Trojan Theater: Space, Vision, and Memory in the Iliad*: 20.
[164] Clay, *Homer's Trojan Theater: Space, Vision, and Memory in the Iliad*: 29.

Jenny Strauss Clay confirms that Homer utilized The Catalogue of Ships, which forms an itinerary, similar a description of Alkinous' palace and the harbor of Phorcys, but on a far grander scale, offers further evidence for a spatial mnemonics.[165] It forms three distinct itineraries that cover a good part of Greece.[166] In the context of the Homeric Formula and the problem of its transmission, J.B. Hainsworth states, Echoes of the Mycenaean Age 1600 – 1150 BCE in Homer's epics are pointed out by John Chadwick, who counts 37 Mycenaean words in the *Iliad* and *Odyssey*.[167] We should not find fault with Homer's imperfect knowledge of the Mycenaean Age as he lived 400 to 500 years after the Trojan War.

---

[165] Clay, *Homer's Trojan Theater: Space, Vision, and Memory in the Iliad*: 117.
[166] Clay, *Homer's Trojan Theater: Space, Vision, and Memory in the Iliad*: 117.
[167] J. B. Hainsworth, "The Homeric Formula & The Problem of its Transmission" by, *Bulletin of the Institute of Classical Studies*, 9:57-68. doi: 10.1111/j.2041-5370.1962. tb00696.x

In fact, historical incidents from the archaeological and linguistic and musicological record show evidence that Homer has preserved the heroic age of Greece, when it was studded with Mycenaean Kingdoms whose influence was felt across the Aegean Sea and Western Anatolia.

The few scant artifacts of bronze, the body shield, the silver studded swords, the tusk helmet, the dove cup and metal inlay still point to the Mycenaean Age.[168] For example, Homer's epic diction, and virtually all the phonological and morphological innovations of the Geometrical Age; are already attested in the epic.[169] In the context of the structure of the Homeric Hexameter, Mark W. Edwards is correct in stating that it is dactylic verse[170] was a South Mycenaean development from 1500 BCE onwards; while the stereotyped stichic hexameter[171] represents a further development in the Ionian branch of the tradition.[172] West postulates that the meter originated in a hemiepes[173] plus a paroemiac.[174]

This was strongly attacked by Hoekstra who points out the difficulties caused for this hypothesis by the juxtaposition of the alternative caesurae.[175] Nagy put forward an alternative theory, that the hexameter arose from a pherecratean pattern expanded by the insertion of three dactyls.[176] Gentili associate the origin of the hexameter with that of dactyloepitrite.[177] I believe that a traditional poetic language leads to the crystallization of metrical formulae, which in turn affect the meter

---

[168] Hainsworth, *Bulletin of the Institute of Classical Studies*:57-68.
[169] Hainsworth, *Bulletin of the Institute of Classical Studies*:57-68.
[170] Dactylic verse: A hexameter consisting of five dactyls and either a spondee or trochee, in which any of the first four dactyls, and sometimes the fifth, may be replaced by a spondee.
[171] Hexameter: a line of verse consisting of six metrical feet. URL: https://www.merriam-webster.com/dictionary/hexameter. 24/8/2018.
[172] Mark W. Edwards, "Homer and Oral Tradition: The Formula", Part I by in *Oral Tradition*, 1 (February, 1986): 171-230. URL: http://www.journal.oraltradition.org/files/articles/1ii/2_edwards.php.
[173] Hemiepes: a dactylic tripody having a spondaic third foot or lacking the two short syllables of the third foot.
[174] Edwards, "Homer's."
[175] Edwards, "Homer's."

[177] Edwards, "Homer's."

and give rise to the caesurae and bridges. For instance, phraseological correspondence between the

Homeric *kleos aphthiton* and Vedic *srava(s) aksitam*, both derive from an Indo-European prototype *klewos ndhg hitom*.[178] Suggestive that a common Indo-European base lay behind the hexameter.

James Notopoulos postulates what I have always believed, after analyzing Hesiod and the Homeric hymns stating that it is a traditional formulaic texture which underlies the epics.[179] More importantly what I always believed from sixth grade through twelve grade in reading Homer in modern Greek katharevousa; Homer was restricted by the use of Greek, as it was spoken between 900 BCE and 700 BCE. For example, Eugene O' Neill analyzes 1000- line samples of the *Iliad*, *Odyssey*, Hesiod, Aratus, Callimachus, Apollonius, and Theocritus and presents statistical data showing that every metrical word type, from shortest to longest has certain avoided positions within the line consistent from poet to poet.[180] In the context of localization or concentration of the vast bulk of words in only a few positions, O'Neill found that localization is as high as 90% in the hexameter of Homer.[181] O'Neill states, 'We confront the impressive fact that the limitations on where the Homeric bard could place his words in his verse were so great as to restrict 86-87% of all his words to less than 40% of their metrically possible positions.[182] He points out that what restricted his use of individual words must have been the traditional language in which he had to cast his verse.[183]

In sum, Homer shows a mastery of the Greek language as it was spoken 2700 years ago. Further, he is free to create by analogy, to invert traditional usages, or to build a verse counter to expectations of his audience if it serves an artistic end. Despite the phenomenon of localization which suggests that nearly all languages is based on existing patterns. This in no way stops Homer from displaying his skill set and a

---

[178] Edwards, "Homer's."
[179] Joseph A. Russo. "A Closer Look at Homeric Formulas." *Transactions and Proceedings of the American Philological Association* 94 (1963): 235-47. URL: http://www.jstor.org/stable/283649 doi: 1.
[180] Russo, "A Closer," 235-47.
[181] Russo, "A Closer," 235-47.
[182] Russo, "A Closer," 235-47.
[183] Russo, "A Closer," 235-47.

personality of a truly gifted oral poet.

How flexible is the formula or systems of formulas used by Homer in his epics? How many different noun epithet combinations does Homer use in his epics? Is this the reason why Homer's epics are considered masterpieces of orality?

Homer's ability to expand or contract the content put into a theme is a recognized part of oral technique.[184] Scholars have noticed that Homer's technique of ornamentations extends' down to the level of the formula.[185] Among noun epithet formulae, four main types of epithet used by Homer are: a) special or confined to one noun; b) generic; c) determinative i.e. a) or b) used of a sub-class within the broadest denotation of the noun and d) functional or not predictable from meter and context.[186]

J. B. Hainsworth, points to how Homer used the dyctalic hexameter. For example, expressions shaped in initial or medial positions in the 1st – 2nd feet.[187] Expressions shaped in 5th – 6th feet with unique expressions; possible formulae and derivative expressions; and regular formulae confined to 5th – 6th feet.[188] Expressions shaped in 1st – 2nd feet with evident unique expressions; possible formulae and derivative expressions and regular formulae confined to 1st – 2nd feet which is also apparent.[189] Hainsworth also identifies expressions shaped in the 2nd – 3rd feet such as unique expressions; possible formulae and derivative expressions and regular formulae confined to 2nd – 3rd feet.[190] Expressions shaped in 4th – 5th feet have unique expressions; possible formulae and derivative expressions and regular formulae confined to 4th – 5th feet.[191] Expressions shaped in 5th – 6th feet show a greater quantity of unique expressions; possible formulae and derivative expressions and regular formulae confined to 5th – 6th feet.[192]

---

[184] J.B. Hainsworth, *The Flexibility of the Homeric Formula*, (Oxford, Clarendon Press, 1968): 74.
[185] J.B. Hainsworth, *The Flexibility of the Homeric Formula*: 74.
[186] J.B. Hainsworth, *The Flexibility of the Homeric Formula*: 75.
[187] J.B. Hainsworth, *The Flexibility of the Homeric Formula*: 131. See Table 1.
[188] Hainsworth, *The Flexibility of the Homeric Formula*: 132-133. See Table II.
[189] Hainsworth, *The Flexibility of the Homeric Formula*: 134. See Table III.
[190] Hainsworth, *The Flexibility of the Homeric Formula*: 134-135. See Table IV.
[191] Hainsworth, *The Flexibility of the Homeric Formula*: 132-133. See Table V.
[192] Hainsworth, *The Flexibility of the Homeric Formula*: 136. See Table VI.

Hainsworth identifies more complex formulae shaped mobile between 1st – 2nd, 2nd – 3rd, 4th-5th, and 5th – 6th feet also in large units.[193] Formulae shaped mobile between 1st – 2nd, 2nd – 3rd, 4th-5th, and 5th-6th feet is also evident.[194] I believe the function of the run-over epithet or division of formulae by the verse end, as a case of enjambement underlies Homer's craft. For example, the function is to add a new idea, either to be expanded by what follows, or to act in some other way as a bond between this and the preceding idea.[195] More importantly, the epithet, being formulaic, persists even when the construction of the noun is changed as in *The Odyssey* 668-9.[196] In the Iliad, Homer's staple is battle.[197] Homer's ability to visualize a scene and knowledge of Mycenaean Society and Culture and insight into people coupled with rhythmic verse lie at the heart of one of the world's greatest poets.

In sum, the formula by analogy or substitution system has replaced but not eliminated the memorized formula in the context of improvising methods. Further, Homer's use of personal names in relation to the comprehensive substitution systems provided by the generic epithets take care of most contingencies. Homer demonstrates a phenomenal memory for names, places, situations, and the dynamic of relationships, kingships, societies, war and peace.

---

[193] Hainsworth, *The Flexibility of the Homeric Formula:* 136. See Table VII.
[194] Hainsworth, *The Flexibility of the Homeric Formula:* 143. See Table XV.
[195] Hainsworth, *The Flexibility of the Homeric Formula:* 105.
[196] Hainsworth, *The Flexibility of the Homeric Formula:* 105.
[197] Hainsworth, *The Flexibility of the Homeric Formula:* 110.

The Rage of Achilles. Copyright Oxford University Press, 2018. All Rights Reserved.

The Poet Singer of Tales in Homer's Iliad and Odyssey. Copyright Houston University, Texas, USA, 2018. All Rights Reserved.

How do we define Singers, Performance and Training from Homer to modern singers of tales? How do they differ in relation to their oral performance and composition of oral tradition?

What is important is not the oral performance but rather the composition during oral performance.[198] From 20 October 1934 to 24 March 1935, Milman Parry and Albert Lord recorded Avdo Mededovic, a 65 year- old Bosnian Muslim, known as the Yugoslav Homer.[199] Avdo Mededovic, an illiterate peasant farmer, sang The Wedding of Smailagic Meho, which runs to over 12,000 lines.[200] Milman Parry tested how Mededovic build on themes, by asking him to listen to another talented singer called Mumin Vlahovljak from Plevlje.[201] Avdo was asked if he could sing Mumin's song, which ran to several thousand lines.[202] Milman Parry describes how, 'Avdo began and as he sang, the song lengthened, the ornamentation and richness accumulated, and the human touches of character, touches that distinguished Avdo from other singers, imparted a depth of feeling that had been missing in Mumin's version'.[203] Avdo was able to expand on Mumin's song by elaboration, by the addition of similes and of telling characterization. Further, through years of practical training, Avdo had also other models in his mind to put his stamp of his own understanding of the heroic mind.[204]

So also did the problem of the variety of dialect and archaic forms in the poems.[205] Peculiarities of language and structure of the Homeric poems or oral poetry. The problem of a mixture of dialects, the archaisms, the repetitions and epic tags and even the manner of composition by addition and expansion of themes.[206]

---

[198] Lord, *The Singer of Tales*: 5.
[199] Lord, *The Singer of Tales*: xi.
[200] Lord, *The Singer of Tales*: 79.
[201] Lord, *The Singer of Tales*: 78.
[202] Lord, *The Singer of Tales*: 78.
[203] Lord, *The Singer of Tales*: 78.
[204] Lord, *The Singer of Tales*: 79.
[205] Lord, *The Singer of Tales*: 11.
[206] Lord, *The Singer of Tales*: 11.

In the context of tradition, W. J. Woodhouse states, 'The *Iliad* seems to be built up from a great mass of legend or tradition historical in form, and professing to be also historical in character and in details'.[207] He identifies disjoined passages in the epics which show that Homer utilized a lost chronicle called the *Saga of Odysseus* and the *Saga of Agamemnon*.[208] The glaring contrast being Agamemnon's return from the fall of Troy to his kingdom Argos, only to be murdered by his treacherous wife.[209] In contrast, Odysseus undergoes many experiences on sea and land to find his kingdom on Ithaca threatened by young suitors. In addition, Penelope, the faithful wife, with the help of her son Telemachus, helps Odysseus, kill all the suitors in the great hall.[210] Penelope is the special favorite of Athene, whose motto is "Endure my heart".[211]

Using the noun verb or noun epithet phrase formula, William Merritt Sale identifies 190 nouns in Homer (113 in the *Iliad*, 77 in the *Odyssey*).[212] He points out that 673 formulae in Homer occur just once, 490 occur twice, 194 occur three times and so on.[213] Sale argues' that Homer has, a system of regular noun epithet nominative formulae that fall in position 9-12; then there are narrower systems defined by the nouns of various shapes that help to make up these formulae, a sub-system for bacchiacs with regular formulae in 9-12; one for monosyllables, one for spondees.[214] William Merritt Sale is correct in stating that such systems were traditional, that no one poet could have devised anything so elaborate in a single lifetime. Furthermore, almost all, of the formulae themselves were traditional and existed before Homer lived.[215]

---

[207] W. J. Woodhouse, *The Composition of Homer's Odyssey,* (Oxford: Clarendon Press, 1969): 17.
[208] Woodhouse, *The Composition of Homer's Odyssey*: 246.
[209] Woodhouse, *The Composition of Homer's Odyssey*: 142.
[210] Woodhouse, *The Composition of Homer's Odyssey*: 170.
[211] Woodhouse, *The Composition of Homer's Odyssey*: 248.
[212] William Merritt Sale, "Homer and the Roland: The Shared Formula Technique," Part II, in *Oral Tradition*, 8/2 (February, 1993): 381-412. URL: http://www.journal.oraltradition.org/files/articles/8ii/7_sale_part.
[213] Sale, "Homer", 381:412.
[214] Sale, "Homer", 381:412.
[215] Sale, "Homer", 381:412.

How many formulae does Homer employ in his epics in total? Noun epithet formulae have come to be regarded as the very staples of Homeric composition.[216] Our characters display a total of 291 once only formulae for 38 characters invented or re-invented by Homer; 197 generic formulae or generic epithets; and 94 distinctive formulae; 13 echoes of the other poem; 4 that repeat parts of long formulae, and the 17 quasi generic formulae. A total of 606 total formulae.[217] Parry's basic theory is that the epithets found in the systems of noun epithets were chosen for the sake of their meter, their color, and their [noble] power, but not their applicability to specific contexts.[218]

How did Homer use the positive and negative attributes of wine to magnify or minimize characters traits in his epics? Wine is used by Homer in a masterful way to portray to an audience mind's eye his characters strengths and flaws. For example, the positive attributes of wine in Homer's epics include:
Physical, revitalizes, helps generate strength, warms the body, slakes thirst, accompaniment to food, pleasant aroma, looks attractive, pleasing taste, life giving, relaxant, and soporific.[219] Psychological, engenders love, brings joy and cheer, provides bravado, alleviates despair, heals grief, frees truth, and excites you.[220] Social, cultivates fellowship, solidifies friendship or drinks to health, marks special occasions, makes oaths and compacts binding, inspires music, singing and dancing, reward for work, conducive to merriment, serves as gift, hospitality for guests, weapon against enemy, reward for valor, celebrate victory, reward for killing enemy and assists in decision making.[221]

Religious, libations, offerings to the gods, attendant in prayer and sacrifice,

---

[216] William Merritt Sale, "The Trojans, Statistics and Milman Parry", *Greek, Roman and Byzantine Studies Library,* last modified May 22, 2016. URL: http://www.grbs.library.duke.edu/article/download/4241/5559 page 341.

[218] Sale, "The Trojans": 364-390.
[219] John Maxwell O'Brien, *Alexander the Great: The Invisible Enemy*, London, Routledge Press, 1992: 234-235.
[220] O'Brien, *Alexander the Great*: 234-235.
[221] O'Brien, *Alexander the Great*: 234-236.

celebrate festivals, spiritual lubricant, honoring the dead, communion with god, and necessary in expiatory rites.[222] Economic, medium of exchange, valuable resource, and drinking vessels and jars valuable commodity.[223] Negative or Physical, Gets' you drunk, and drains your strength.[224] Negative Psychological effects, affects your memory, drives you mad, fogs your mind, evokes violence, leads to lust, is an enemy, and brings out bestiality.[225] Social, can leave you in ruin.[226] Religious, Dionysus can make you do things.[227]

How does Homer use digressions to achieve a desired effect? How does Homer use similes to outline character and plot? For example, to show a thematic contrast or to mark a shifting scene? How does Homer use simile as a direct focus on a single theme and the use of parallel similemes to create a unified theme? How does Homer use similes to interpret typical actions? Does Homer use similes as guides through a series of type scenes? Does Homer use similes for complexity? Is Homer a creative poet and does the audience co-create in the re-telling of his epics?

Homer utilized a vast storehouse of similes to convey in his audience's mind's eye, aesthetic qualities. For example, they describe scenes of Greek life such as landscapes and seascapes; storms and calm weather, fighting among animals, civic disputes, athletic contests, horse races, community entertainment, women involved in their daily tasks, men running farms and orchards.[228] Homer used expository digressions widely and effectively in telling his stories and how the similes can be approached as parallel narrative devices.[229]

For example, William C. Scott points to Book 8 of the Odyssey. Similes are long digressions. The poet creates a strong break from the locale of the ongoing narrative for digressions that develop their own stories in response to their own motivations.[230] Homer appears to have inherited a long tradition of poet

---

[222] O'Brien, *Alexander the Great*: 234-236.
[223] O'Brien, *Alexander the Great*: 234-236.
[224] O'Brien, *Alexander the Great*: 234-237.
[225] O'Brien, *Alexander the Great*: 234-237.
[226] O'Brien, *Alexander the Great*: 234-237.
[227] O'Brien, *Alexander the Great*: 234-237.
[228] William C. Scott, *The Artistry of the Homeric Simile*, Lebanon, Dartmouth College Press, 2009: Preface.
[229] Scott, *The Artistry of the Homeric Simile*: 2.
[230] Scott, *The Artistry of the Homeric Simile*: 4.

– audience performances of epics, which enabled him to make choices in shaping his similes to support the narrative.[231] For example, both Milman Parry, his successors and critics point to the special nature and extent of formulaic expression in a performance environment.[232] Others have focused on repeated typological scenes.[233] I believe William C. Scott is correct in stating that, before Homer there was a group of bards composing songs that kept alive tales from earlier centuries'.[234]

In doing so, they continually molded and honed their language to make it a highly expressive tool.[235] William C. Scott provides insight into the working of Homer's mind in stating that both long and short similes are a result of a complex process that requires the participation of both poet and audience.[236] In the context of Homer's use of similes to delineate character and plot, It seems certain that Homer did not invent his major characters, rather, he repeatedly borrows them from earlier tales by accommodating and adapting their salient traits to the needs of his continuing narrative.[237] For example, the most frequent similes are to describe his warriors. Achilles is Ares, the helmeted god of war; a fire; a sun; a bird of prey; a hunting dog; a lion and a wolf.[238] Homer also uses similes to delineate a narrative theme. For example, Homer develops the motif of the gods' anger against the wall's builders.

Specifically, the description of the wall; the introduction of Hector as leader of the Trojans; the frustrated attack of Asios; the general battle stressing the successful resistance of the Greeks and the determination of Hector.[239] Homer uses thematic similes to reassure his audience also. For example, in book 5 of the Odyssey, Odysseus leaves the comfortable island of Calypso; and seeks a world of death, sickness, a flawed world dominated by powerful and often vindictive divinities.[240]

---

[231] Scott, *The Artistry of the Homeric Simile*: 14.
[232] Scott, *The Artistry of the Homeric Simile*: 14.
[233] Scott, *The Artistry of the Homeric Simile*: 14.
[234] Scott, *The Artistry of the Homeric Simile*: 15.
[235] Scott, *The Artistry of the Homeric Simile*: 15.
[236] Scott, *The Artistry of the Homeric Simile*: 42.
[237] Scott, *The Artistry of the Homeric Simile*: 42.
[238] Scott, *The Artistry of the Homeric Simile*: 74.
[239] Scott, *The Artistry of the Homeric Simile*: 95.
[240] Scott, *The Artistry of the Homeric Simile*: 118.

Despite Odysseus' trials and difficulties; he is compelled to build his own raft, and earn his way relying on his own wits.[241] Despite the threats to our hero, Zeus declares that Odysseus is fated to see his friends and to return to his palace on Ithaca.[242] Homer uses a powerful simile to delineate the actions of men on the battlefield; and the action of the Gods of Olympus on the battlefield.[243] Specifically, to Zeus' plan to honor Achilles in book 13; relates to his promise to Thetis on book 1 and his commands to the Olympians in book 8.[244]

---

[241] Scott, *The Artistry of the Homeric Simile*: 118.
[242] Scott, *The Artistry of the Homeric Simile*: 118.
[243] Scott, *The Artistry of the Homeric Simile*: 138.
[244] Scott, *The Artistry of the Homeric Simile*: 138.

How does Homer use the word *amymon* to describe a hero or person in his epics? How is Homer's vocabulary viewed by scholars?

I agree with Aristarchus who said that the epithets of Homer are ornamental.[245] Critical analysis of Homer's epithets reveal that they are not ordinarily chosen for their special relevance to the immediate context.[246] Furthermore, since the great majority of epithets are honorific, and since epithets are roughly interchangeable and can be selected according to metrical needs.[247] *Amymon* means blameless.[248] *Amymon*, or blameless, is used by Homer 116 times in his epics.[249]

Of the sixty- five times that the adjective is used in the Iliad, it refers to people in all but nine instances.[250] Of the fifty- one times that it is used in the Odyssey, it refers to people in all but twelve instances or thirty- nine times.[251] *Momos* originally meant a physical flaw or blemish on the assumption that a concrete meaning probably preceded an abstract one.[252] There are forty- three characters in the Iliad except Achilles, called *amynon*.[253] Achilles is called *amymon* thirteen times.[254]

There are ten instances in which the use of *amymon* with nouns denoting an activity or profession is used.[255] Homer uses *Amymon* with nouns not denoting persons twenty times and three anomalous times in the Odyssey.[256] Characters who are compared to gods occurs twenty- six times in the *Iliad* and thirty- one times in the *Odyssey*.[257] Anne Amory Parry demonstrates that all these epithets glorify warriors and can therefore be used interchangeably as the meter demands or as a

---

[245] Anne Amory Parry, *Amymon and Other Homeric Epithets,* Leiden, E. J. Brill Publishers,   1973: 2.
[246] Parry, *Amymon and Other Homeric Epithets:* 3.
[247] Parry, *Amymon and Other Homeric Epithets:* 3.
[248] Parry, *Amymon and Other Homeric Epithets:* 10.
[249] Parry, *Amymon and Other Homeric Epithets:* 6.
[250] Parry, *Amymon and Other Homeric Epithets:* 10.
[251] Parry, *Amymon and Other Homeric Epithets:* 10.
[252] Parry, *Amymon and Other Homeric Epithets:* 35.
[253] Parry, *Amymon and Other Homeric Epithets:* 171.
[254] Parry, *Amymon and Other Homeric Epithets:* 172.
[255] Parry, *Amymon and Other Homeric Epithets:* 173.
[256] Parry, *Amymon and Other Homeric Epithets:* 173-174.
[257] Parry, *Amymon and Other Homeric Epithets:* 222-223.

desire for variety suggests.[258] To Homer and his audience a sense of precision and

---

[258] Parry, *Amymon and Other Homeric Epithets:* 164.

relevance, a pleasure in the right use of language came not as it does for us from the special relevance of an adjective to a given situation or action, but from the distinctive connotations of each adjective. In sum, Homer's recurrent ornamental epithets have the advantage of being eternally relevant to the heroic character and tradition because they all refer to qualities that were considered most important in the tradition; seen through the eyes of Homer.

How does Musike relate to Oral Tradition as a Living Tradition in Greek Culture?

Thrasybulos Georgiades argues that the Greek language is the bearer of meaning and has a musical component.[259] He outlines the distinguishing characteristic of ancient Greek lies in the realization of the word as an independent rhythmic musical force and at the same time as language, as a phonetic structure, as a vehicle of perceptions and affections.[260] In the context of Homeric verse and the use of the dactylic hexameter, I agree with Th. Georgiades who states, that the duration of the long syllable was not to be considered exact, that the proportion of duration between longs and shorts was only approximate, and that, finally, there was no strict rhythm and that the verse was to be recited more like the spoken word in a modern sense.[261] A second possible component is an ancient Greek round dance; the *syrtos kalamatianos*, attested by ancient rhythmic theorists.[262] It is a rhythm which consists of three counts, in which the first is longer by one half than the second and third.[263] A characteristic of this dance is the give and take; or standing still and pressing forward.[264] As one dances this round, one feels the elastic quality of this rhythm, but at the same time the static loose juxtaposition of the individual temporal units.[265]

An inscription from Boethia dating from the first century [CE] reads: "He devoutly arranged festival processions in the tradition of his fathers and the traditional round

---

[259] Thrasybulos Georgiades, translated by Erwin Benedikt and Marie Louis Martinez, *Greek Music, Verse and Dance*, New York, Da Capo Press, 1955: 93.
[260] Georgiades, *Greek Music, Verse and Dance*: 99.
[261] Georgiades, *Greek Music, Verse and Dance*: 132.
[262] Georgiades, *Greek Music, Verse and Dance*: 134.
[263] Georgiades, *Greek Music, Verse and Dance*: 134.
[264] Georgiades, *Greek Music, Verse and Dance*: 135.
[265] Georgiades, *Greek Music, Verse and Dance*: 135.

dance of the *syrtoi*".[266] Georgiades argues, that one could call to mind the Delian chorus *geranos* and the description of this dance by Homer himself in the 18th song of the *Iliad*.[267] The dancers convey a primeval tradition which has been deeply stamped, as it were, upon their very souls; their reverence for their forefathers and their unity with them become manifest.[268] Besides, tracing the hexameter to the rhythm of the *syrtos kalamatianos* poses the question as to what extent the epics was originally related to dance? We can imagine the dancing of the Phaeaces to the chant of Demodokos in the Odyssey, 8th song, in epic hexameter.[269] It may have been possible to sing the epics and at the same time to dance it. Two instruments which may have formed part of Homeric verse and performance is the *aulos* wind instrument and the *phorminx* stringed instrument. Georgiades argues that the *aulos* is capable, of expressing something similar to that, which is revealed by the voice; it can assume an attitude related to the expression of affections.[270] For example, the goddess Athena was so deeply impressed by the mourning of Euryales, the sister of Medusa, that she preserved it; as cries of mourning, representing the *aulos* tune.[271] Probably one reed produced bourdon tones, similar to those of the bagpipe.[272] The *phorminx*, has the phenomenon of consonance and is the very basis of lyre playing.[273]

In sum, Homer may have employed musicians to highlight key themes, characters, battles, war and peace. The function of Homer as bard is to entertain and educate his audiences, using a monumental structure from oral tradition and ethos, inherited from the Mycenaean Age.

---

[266] Georgiades, *Greek Music, Verse and Dance*: 136.
[267] Georgiades, *Greek Music, Verse and Dance*: 137.
[268] Georgiades, *Greek Music, Verse and Dance*: 140.
[269] Georgiades, *Greek Music, Verse and Dance*: 141.
[270] Georgiades, *Greek Music, Verse and Dance*: 40-41.
[271] Georgiades, *Greek Music, Verse and Dance*: 41.
[272] Georgiades, *Greek Music, Verse and Dance*: 44.
[273] Georgiades, *Greek Music, Verse and Dance*: 45.

Exekias' Ajax and Achilles Playing a Game. Copyright Metropolitan Museum, New York, United States of America, 2018. All Rights Reserved.

Heracles and the Gods on Mount Olympus. Copyright the *Times* Israel, 2018. All Rights Reserved.

What musical instruments may have been used in Mycenaean Courts by poets between 1600 –1150 BCE in relation to Homer's epics? The Hellenic *aulos* with two straight pipes of equal length always remained distinct from its supposed ancestor the Phrygian *aulos*, one of whose pipes ended in a joint that was either curved or made of horn, hence its Greek name.[274] According to Aristoxenus (in Athenaeus, *Sophists at Dinner*, xiv.36) there were four categories covering 'more than three octaves'; from the highest to the lowest auloi they are the parthenian ('of young girls'), the 'childlike' (*paidikoi*), auloi to accompany the kithara (*kithariatērioi*), the 'perfect' (*teleioi*) and the 'more than perfect' (*huperteleioi*), the two last-named being also grouped under the term 'masculine' (*andreioi*).[275]

This classification by range has no bearing upon the practical use, material, origin or form of the instrument.[276] Yet, its terminology goes hand in hand with certain terms known from other sources in connection with musical practice: 'Pythian *aulos*', suitable for playing the *nomos* of the same name and described as 'virile' (thus placing it among the *auloi teleioi*); '*kitharist auloi*', that is, *auloi* played with the *kithara* or an instrument of the same register; and the much-discussed *aulos magadis*, about which Greek scholars cannot agree, although it is likely that it had qualities similar to the *magadis*, a kind of harp capable of playing octaves.[277] The *phorminx* of the Mycenaean Greeks, as works of art attest, was a lyre with a shallow wooden sound-box with a rounded base, similar in most details to the earlier lyre of Minoan Crete and, like it, having two arms that often curved in and out in an ornamental fashion, supporting a crossbar to which seven strings were fixed with leather strips (*kollopes*) for friction.[278] The instrument was held upright, and played in the same manner as the later kithara.[279]

---

[274] *Aulos,* by Annie Belis, Accessed 29/4/2016 URL:http://www.oxfordmusiconline.com.ezp.lib.unimelb.edu.au/subscriber/article/grove/music /01532?q=Aulos.
[275] Anne Belis, *Aulos,*: 1.
[276] Anne Belis, *Aulos:* 1.
[277] Anne Belis, *Aulos:* 1.
[278] Martha Mass, *Phorminx,* URL:http://www.oxfordmusiconline.com.ezp.lib.unimelb.edu.au/subscriber/article/grove/music /21597? Accessed 29/4/2016.
[279] Martha Mass, Phorminx: 1.

In sum, musicians and bards at Mycenaean Courts combined in both simple and complex fashion to entertain powerful nobles and to provide insight into human nature.

What formula did Homer employ in relation to epic poetry?

The defining marks of formulaic technique and of thematic structure in both poems, of 27,000 lines is truly amazing.[280] Albert Lord points to the subtlety and intricacy of the Greek hexameter.[281] The Greek hexameter allows for greater variety, because the line may be broken at more than one place by a caesura.[282] The caesura can occur in any one of the following points in the line: a) after the first syllable of the third foot, b) after the second syllable of the third foot if it is a dactyl, and c) after the first syllable of the fourth foot. To these should be added d) the bucolic diaeresis (after the fourth foot) and e) the pause after a run over word at the beginning of the line, which occurs most frequently after the first syllable of the second foot.[283]

Milman Parry's analysis reveals formulas of one foot and a half, two feet and a half, two feet and three quarters, three feet and a half, four feet, and six feet in length measured from the beginning of the line, and complementary lengths measured from the pause to the end of the line.[284] In effect, the formula technique in the Homeric poems, is so perfect, the system of formulas Parry alluded to, so thrifty, so lacking in identical alternative expressions, that one marvels that this perfection could be reached without the aid of writing.[285] In sum, Homer combined a long tradition; with varying degrees of speed before a live audience, using a lost art of hexameter formula.

---

[280] Lord, *The Singer of Tales*: 142.
[281] Lord, *The Singer of Tales*: 142.
[282] Lord, *The Singer of Tales*: 142.
[283] Lord, *The Singer of Tales*: 142.
[284] Lord, *The Singer of Tales*: 142.
[285] Lord, *The Singer of Tales*: 144.

Odysseus and a Siren. URL: https://www.pinterest.com.au/helenepoulakou/homers-odyssey/ Accessed 2/7/2018.

Fight over Patroclus. Copyright Oxford University Press, 2018. All Rights Reserved.

What major and minor themes make up the *Iliad & The Odyssey*?

Albert Lord confirms that the architectonics of thematic structure in the poems are wondrous to observe.[286] For example, the relationship between the three examples of the assembly theme in Book I could be expressed as a) the assembly called by Achilles, b) the assembly of the gods, and c) the quarrel between Chryses and Agamemnon.[287] We see an overlapping of themes, or more precisely, the way in which minor themes are useful in more than one major theme.[288] In effect, the first two books of the *Iliad* reveal seven examples of the assembly theme.[289] In the analysis of the poems, I am becoming aware of Homer's interweaving and over-lapping of major themes; and begin to glimpse the complexity of thematic structure in the *Iliad*.[290] In effect, Homer embodies a tradition, he is one of the integral parts of that complex.[291] For his audiences, Homer's vividness and immediacy arise from the fact that he is a practicing oral poet.[292]

---

[286] Lord, *The Singer of Tales*: 146.
[287] Lord, *The Singer of Tales*: 146.
[288] Lord, *The Singer of Tales*: 146.
[289] Lord, *The Singer of Tales*: 146.
[290] Lord, *The Singer of Tales*: 147.
[291] Lord, *The Singer of Tales*: 147.
[292] Lord, *The Singer of Tales*: 147.

What defines songs and the song?

When the singer of tales, equipped with a store of formulas and themes and a technique of composition takes his place before an audience and tells his story, he follows the plan which he has learned along with the other elements of his profession.[293]

What distinction can we make from Written and Oral Tradition? Milman Parry's distinction of Homeric poetry as an oral tradition is proven, along the following parameters. a) to what extent an oral poet who composes a new poem is dependent upon the traditional poetry in whole for his phraseology, his scheme of composition, and the thought of his poem, b) to what extent a poem, original or traditional, is stable in successive recitations of a given singer, c) how a poem is changed given locality over many years, d) how it is changed. Furthermore, its travels from one region to another. In what ways a given poem travels from one region to another. And the extent to which the poetry travels. The different sources of the material from which a given heroic cycle is created. The factors that determine the creation, growth, and decline of the heroic cycle. The relation of the events of an historical cycle to the actual events. ix.[294] Milman Parry and Albert Lord are correct in stating somewhat reservedly, that the art of narrative song was perfected, long before the advent of writing.[295] Robinson states that the Mycenaeans used a form of script written in the Greek language, known now as Linear B.[296] Eighty-nine characters make up Linear B, 48 of which can be traced back to Minoan writing, Linear A, probably originated in the simple pictographic script of the earliest Minoans.[297] In addition, the chief tans who ruled over the walled fortresses of Mycenae were buried in spectacular graves that contained weapons adorned with copper and gold as well as fine gold face masks modeled in the likeness of their owners.[298] More

---

[293] Lord, *The Singer of Tales*: 99.
[294] Lord, *The Singer of Tales:* 124.
[295] Lord, *The Singer of Tales*: 124.
[296] Brian M. Fagan, *People of the Earth: An Introduction to World Prehistory*, New York: Longman, 1998: 488.
[297] Fagan, *People of the Earth*, 1998: 488.
[298] Fagan, *People of the Earth*, 1998: 486.

importantly for an insight into the Homeric epics, the wealth and economic power of the Mycenaeans came from their trading contacts and from their warrior skills.[299]

In sum, the Greek Kings of the Mycenaean Age, inspired bards or poets to immortalize their deeds on the battle field, their ethics, their values and courage which shine through Homer's epics.

Telemachus and Nestor. Copyright Oxford University Press, 2018. All Rights Reserved.

---

[299] Fagan, *People of the Earth*, 1998: 486.

How did Homer apply his use of the Greek language in his oral recitations of the *Iliad* and the *Odyssey* before aristocratic banquets, festivals or market places?

The most astute observation by Milman Parry in relation to the style of the Homeric poems led him to understand that so highly formulaic a style could only be traditional.[300] Who acts as a reoccurring nexus between Olympus and the world of men, in the context of the heroic code? The theme of divine protection of a human favorite is a constant element of Homer's.[301] G.S. Kirk points out that this is characteristic of early Greek traditional epic poetry which existed before the *Odyssey*.[302]

For example, Tydeus was constantly helped by Athene, Nestor singled her out in his prayers, and Hera loved and protected Jason.[303] I believe that Mycenaean Greeks trading with Assyria and the Hittite Empire,[304] may have heard the Epic of Gilgamesh, the well-known king of Uruk circa 2700- 2600 BCE.[305] N. K. Sandars states, 'It would have been historically possible for the poet of the *Odyssey* to hear the story of Gilgamesh not garbled but direct for ships from Ionia and the [Aegean Islands] who were already trading on the Syrian coast.[306] The oldest version of the epic was written down in 2100 BCE.[307] Sumerian epic was probably the creation of proto-literate phase of archaic Sumerian civilization at about 3000 BCE.[308] The hero of the epic Gilgamesh is two parts god and one- part man, for his mother was a goddess like the mother of Achilles. A tragic hero at the center of a conflict between the desires of the god and the destiny of man.[309]

---

[300] Lord, *The Singer of Tales*: 11.
[301] G. S. Kirk, *Homer and The Epic: A Shortened Version of The Songs of Homer*, Cambridge, Cambridge University Press, 1976: 224.
[302] Kirk, *Homer and The Epic:* 224.
[303] Kirk, *Homer and The Epic:* 224.
[304] N. K. Sandars, translator, *The Epic of Gilgamesh*, Harmondsworth, Penguin Books, 1972: 46.
[305] Sandars, *The Epic of Gilgamesh:* 20.
[306] Sandars, *The Epic of Gilgamesh:* 45.
[307] Sandars, *The Epic of Gilgamesh:* 17.
[308] Sandars, *The Epic of Gilgamesh:* 19.
[309] Sandars, *The Epic of Gilgamesh:* 21.

The Epic of Gilgamesh is a poem in 12 songs of about 300 lines each, inscribed on separate tablets.[310] Despite its primitive features of repetition and stock epithet; the language is not at all naïve or primitive; on the contrary, it is elaborately wrought.[311] These epithets are less frequent than those attached to Hector or Odysseus.[312] Put succinctly, the Sumerian and Semitic versions have a word for word repetition of long passages of narrative or conversation, and of elaborate greeting formulae.[313] These are familiar characteristics of oral poetry, tending to assist the task of the reciter, also to give satisfaction to the audience.[314]

In sum, oral poetry is a vibrant, eclectic, highly developed art form, passed down from a long line of experienced bards or poets who played a key role in transmitting culture from generation to generation.

---

[310] Sandars, *The Epic of Gilgamesh*: 47.
[311] Sandars, *The Epic of Gilgamesh*: 47.
[312] Sandars, *The Epic of Gilgamesh*: 48.
[313] Sandars, , *The Epic of Gilgamesh*: 48.
[314] Sandars, , *The Epic of Gilgamesh*: 48.

Why does Aristotle hold Homer in such high regard? What insight does Aristotle give to the Homeric Epics and how does he respond to critics in the Homeric Problem?

From what we can glean from Aristotle's 202 extant works[315], Homer is used on many occasions to qualify an assertion or conclusion. For example, a remedy applied to bruised warriors is to apply *thapsia* and metal ladles, which he qualifies with, as the poet says, 'Between his teeth the chilly bronze he bit'.[316] Aristotle refers to Homer as the poet of poets, standing alone not only through the excellence, but also through the dramatic character of his imitations.[317] Aristotle is correct in stating that epic poetry is imitation of serious subjects in meter.[318] Aristotle provides insight into the compositional methods of Homer, stating that the elements of tragedy include spectacle, character, plot, diction, melody, and thought.[319] Tragedy also has a) the complex tragedy, which is all reversal and discovery; b) the tragedy of suffering i.e. Ajax; c) the tragedy of character; d) a scene in the nether world.[320] Aristotle argues that Homer's marvelous superiority lies not only his ability to maximize or minimize characters and plots; but as a master of the metaphor and ornamentation.[321] Aristotle himself asserts, 'His two poems are each examples of construction, the *Iliad* simple and a story of suffering, the *Odyssey* complex and a story of character.[322]

For Aristotle, Homer's superiority lies not only in the fact that he focused on the tenth year of the Trojan War; but in his mastery of the subtlety and intricacy of the Greek language in threading meaningful episodes, which make up the epic.[323] Homer had the ability to make his audience see, what he wanted them to see. And that is a vivid picture of a Heroic Age of Mycenaean Greek Kingdoms and its

---

[315] Jonathan Barnes Ed. *The Complete Works of Aristotle* 2 volumes, Princeton, Princeton University Press, 1984: 2386-2388.
[316] Barnes, *The Complete Works of Aristotle*: 1377.
[317] Barnes, *The Complete Works of Aristotle*: 2318.
[318] Barnes, *The Complete Works of Aristotle*: 2319.
[319] Barnes, *The Complete Works of Aristotle*: 2320.
[320] Barnes, *The Complete Works of Aristotle*: 2330.
[321] Barnes, *The Complete Works of Aristotle*: 2335.
[322] Barnes, *The Complete Works of Aristotle*: 2336.
[323] Barnes, *The Complete Works of Aristotle* 2 volumes: 2335.

place in the world. Aristotle had a deep veneration of Homer and his penetrating insight into the nature of early Hellenic society.[324] The reason why he does so is because Homer excels every other epic poet not only because the *Iliad* and in the *Odyssey* he takes an action that is a unity, but also because he is aware of the part to be played by the poet himself in the poem.[325] For example, in the *Politics* Aristotle's treatment of kingship illumines and is illumined by Homer.[326] Since kingship is a kind of fatherhood, and patriarchy a form of monarchy, the poet is praised for calling Zeus the king of gods or father of men and gods.[327] Zeus's place in the political system of Olympus resembles that of Agamemnon, "shepherd of the people", in the *Iliad*.[328] Martin Nilsson provides a worthy analogy, 'Zeus has full power by right of inheritance, as has Agamemnon.

The other gods appear as his retainers whom he summons to counsel or to meals, just as Agamemnon summons the chiefs. Just as the war king summons the army assembly, so Zeus summons twice an assembly of the gods, in which even the lesser gods, the rivers and the nymphs of the springs and meadows, take part'.[329] More importantly, Aristotle points to words, not found in our texts of Homer, and he shows that the powers of the king of Mycenae in the fighting resembled those of the Spartan kings, who during campaigns had the right to punish with death acts of cowardice on the battlefield,[330] thus defining a true warrior, fights to the finish. More importantly, Aristotle is a truly sensitive interpreter of Homer because of his ability to imagine the poet and the heroes of the poetry in a real world of men, things and events.[331]

---

[324] Historical Criticism in Aristotle's "Homeric Questions", by G. L. Huxley, *Proceedings of the Royal Irish Academy*. Section C: Archaeology, Linguistics, Literature, Vol. 79 (1979), pp.73-81. Published by: Royal Irish Academy, URL: http://www.jstor.org/stable/25506363. Accessed: 22/05/2016.

[325] Historical Criticism in Aristotle's "Homeric Questions", by G. L. Huxley, *Proceedings of the Royal Irish Academy*. Section C: Archaeology, Linguistics, Literature, Vol. 79 (1979), pp.73-81. Published by: Royal Irish Academy, URL: http://www.jstor.org/stable/25506363. Accessed: 22/05/2016.

[326] Huxley, G. L. "Historical Criticism in Aristotle's "Homeric Questions"" *Proceedings of the Royal Irish Academy. Section C: Archaeology, Celtic Studies, History, Linguistics, Literature* 79 (1979): 73-81. http://www.jstor.org/stable/25506363.

[327] Huxley, G. L. "Historical Criticism in Aristotle's "Homeric Questions"":73-81.

[328] Huxley, G. L. "Historical Criticism in Aristotle's "Homeric Questions"":73-81.

[329] Huxley, G. L. "Historical Criticism in Aristotle's "Homeric Questions"":73-81.

[330] Huxley, G. L. "Historical Criticism in Aristotle's "Homeric Questions"":73-81.

[331] Huxley, G. L. "Historical Criticism in Aristotle's "Homeric Questions"":73-81.

Ancient and Modern Critics & Admirers of Homer & the Homeric Question. Homer's poems, the earliest surviving works of Greek literature, contain occasional references to what were later to become scientific and philosophical topics. The poems presuppose a certain vague conception of the nature and origins of the universe and that conception finds echoes, both verbal and substantial in Pre-Socratic thought.[332] Hesiod in his *Theogony* from the 700 BCE century is reflective of this tradition, in which he states:

> Hail, children of Zeus, grant a sweet song and celebrate the holy race of the immortals who exist forever, ...Tell me this, you Muses who have your home on Olympus, from the beginning, and tell which of them first came into being.[333]

In effect, it is the Muses who grant the gift of oral poetry and the poet, who then transmits the epic tradition. Plato states, 'If Homer did no public service, is he said to have become during his lifetime an educational leader in private, with pupils who loved him for his company and who handed down a Homeric way of life to their successors'.[334] Xenophanes of Colophon is critical of Homer, stating, 'Homer ... attributed to the gods all the things which among men are shameful and blameworthy – theft and adultery and mutual deception'.[335] He draws a line between Homer's Olympian pantheon and the one true God, 'There is one God, greatest among gods and men, to mortals neither in shape nor in thought'.[336] Heraclitus 504 BCE from Ephesus, criticized Homer for the violence in his epics. Saying, 'Homer deserved to be thrown out of the games [sixty ninth Olympiad 504/501 BCE] and flogged'.[337] Heraclitus also believed Homer was an astronomer based on the lines [*Iliad* XVIII 251] and [*Iliad* VI 488].[338] The geographer Strabo states, ' Homer calls the arctic circle the

---

[332] Jonathan Barnes, *Early Greek Philosophy*, London, Penguin Books, 1987: 55.
[333] Barnes, *Early Greek Philosophy*: 55.
[334] Barnes, *Early Greek Philosophy*: 84.
[335] Barnes, *Early Greek Philosophy*: 95.
[336] Barnes, *Early Greek Philosophy*: 95.
[337] Barnes, *Early Greek Philosophy*: 105.
[338] Barnes, *Early Greek Philosophy*: 111.

bear',[339] and [the] Limits of morning and evening are the bear and, opposite the bear, the boundary of bright Zeus'.[340]

Criticism and praise for Homer from the East provide us with a balanced picture of the singer of tales. R. C. Prasad argues biased in my opinion, that for Homer the tale was the thing; Homer's thin and accidental characterization; and Homer loses heart i.e. Nausicaa, appears dramatically for only a few lines, like a woman, then she fades, unused.[341] R. C. Prasad argues that the central family in Homer's epics include the sly cattish wife, that coldblooded egotist Odysseus, and the priggish son who yet met his master prig in Menelaus.[342] In praise for Homer, R. C. Prasad states that Homer loved the rural scene and learned the good points of greenwood tree.[343] Further, that Homer sprinkles tags of epic across his pages.[344] He argues that, the technique of the oral epic is largely that of improvisation and the constant epithets, the repeated line; and blocks of lines, the copious store of synonyms and of alternative word forms, are a heritage from improvisation.[345] So, who are the poets who belong, not merely to their own race and language but to the world? I believe Homer fits the following answer by T.S. Elliot: the true sage is rarer than the true poet; and when the two fits, that of wisdom and that of poetic speech, are found in the same man, you have the great poet. It is poets of this kind who belong, not merely to their own people but to the world.[346]

---

[339] Barnes, *Early Greek Philosophy*: 124.
[340] Barnes, *Early Greek Philosophy*: 124.
[341] R. C. Prasad, *Tulasidasa's Shriramacharitamanasa (The Holy Lake of the Acts of Rama)*, New Delhi, Motilal Banarsidass Publishers, 1990: xix.
[342] Prasad, *(The Holy Lake of the Acts of Rama)*: xix.
[343] Prasad, *(The Holy Lake of the Acts of Rama)*: xix.
[344] Prasad, *(The Holy Lake of the Acts of Rama)*: xix.
[345] Prasad, *(The Holy Lake of the Acts of Rama)*: xxi.
[346] Prasad, *(The Holy Lake of the Acts of Rama)*: xxii.

When was Homer's Iliad & The Odyssey composed? How many lines of hexameter verse does it contain? What daily training did Homer most likely undertake to memorize so many verses? Robert Fagles states that the [*Iliad*] consists in the original Greek of 15,693 lines of hexameter verse, composed probably in the late eighth or early seventh century BCE by ... Homer.[347] The Odyssey consists in the original Greek of 12,109 lines of hexameter verse, composed by probably in the late eighth or early seventh century BCE by ... Homer.[348]

I believe Homer belonged to a talented school for singer of tales, whose line goes back to the Mycenaean civilization 1600 – 1150 BCE which echoes in his epics. Homer also acquired a sound knowledge of the Genealogy of the Royal House of Troy.[349] And the Genealogy of the Royal House of Odysseus.[350] Homer's epics are a strong pointer to a period of Greek prehistory when the country was organized into strong kingdoms centering around Mycenae.[351] My father took us to Mycenae, Tiryns and Pylos in July 1986 and walked me through the Lions Gate. Pointing to the East, my father with full conviction said, "The Mycenaean Kings from their seat of power, influenced Asia Minor. The Trojan War was real. The Mycenaean Kingdoms on the Greek mainland were real".

---

[347] Robert Fagles, translator, *Homer: The Iliad*, New York: Penguin Group, 1990: 5.
[348] Fagles, *Homer: The Odyssey*: 3.
[349] Fagles, *Homer: The Iliad*: 617.
[350] Fagles, Homer: The Iliad: 497.
[351] John Chadwick, *The Deciperment of Linear B*, Cambridge, Cambridge University Press, 1990:   6.

Is there tradition and design in Homer's epics? How does the hexameter operate in Homer's epics?

C. M. Bowra argues that Homer inherited his language from his predecessors, who accessed a common pool of ancient stories.[352] For example, Homer assumes his hearers already know about the siege of Troy, and many other events in the heroic history of Greece.[353] He makes passing mention of the famous heroes of an older generation, of Perseus, Daedalus, Theseus and Peirithous.[354]

Ancient Greeks loved the Achaean Catalogue; its lists of heroes; number of Greek ships 1,186; Thucydides' estimate of 100,000 troops for the Siege of Troy.[355] It is addressed to the Muse and a statement of the greatness of the theme.[356] For them it was history, sanctified by tradition, and they demanded it from their poet.[357] The Achaean heroes are the foremost warriors in a great undertaking opposed to Trojan enemies.[358] The Achaean Catalogue also serves as a visual device; to reveal the main Greek heroes; and Trojan opponents; magnifying and minimizing characters with supporting or opposing Olympian Gods behind the scenes.

---

[352] C. M. Bowra, *Tradition and Design in the Iliad*, Oxford: Oxford University Press, 1963: 7.
[353] Bowra, *Tradition and Design in the Iliad*: 5.
[354] Bowra, *Tradition and Design in the Iliad*: 5.
[355] Bowra, *Tradition and Design in the Iliad*: 71.
[356] Bowra, *Tradition and Design in the Iliad*: 70.
[357] Bowra, *Tradition and Design in the Iliad*: 71.
[358] Bowra, *Tradition and Design in the Iliad*: 72.

Does the phorminx played by Demodocus in the Odyssey[359] provide a clue to music and meter in the epics? C. M. Bowra argues that recitation to the lyre was the method of recitation known to him and practiced by him.[360] Homeric verse with its great variations of rhythm and scansion can only have been intoned or sung to a very simple chant.[361] The most notable feature of the Homeric hexameter is the way it preserves its dactylic rhythm.[362] A long syllable may be substituted for two shorts, but two shorts may not be substituted for a long.[363] It allows spondees but not anapaests.[364] In this it differs from some other Greek verse. Anapaestic verse, for instance allows the use of dactyls and spondees as well as anapaests, and so achieves a very varied character which is often far from anapaestic.[365] But the hexameter keeps its dactylic character throughout.[366] I believe the hexameter can be traced to shorter lines used for dactylic tetrameter and dactylic pentameter. Wilamowitz asserts, 'on the analogy of all surviving Greek meters it is hard to believe that so long a verse of sixteen or seventeen syllables should have been a complete unity from the beginning'.[367]

In addition, Homeric verse shows a strong predilection for a break after the fourth foot.[368] K. Witte provides an insight into Homer's mind in using the hexameter, stating that the original form was a dactylic tetrameter followed by a dactylic dimeter catalectic.[369] This view is supported by evidence in Homer's dislike of spondees in the fourth foot.[370] In the Iliad there are only 280 spondees in the fourth foot, a small proportion in so long a poem.[371] In effect, the Homeric caesura is due to the two original elements being formed into a single hexameter.[372] In practice, Homer adhered to strict rules which keep the epic intact and separate and employs

---

[359] Bowra, *Tradition and Design in the Iliad*: 53.
[360] Bowra, *Tradition and Design in the Iliad*: 54.
[361] Bowra, *Tradition and Design in the Iliad*: 58.
[362] Bowra, *Tradition and Design in the Iliad*: 61.
[363] Bowra, *Tradition and Design in the Iliad*: 62.
[364] Bowra, *Tradition and Design in the Iliad*: 62.
[365] Bowra, *Tradition and Design in the Iliad*: 62.
[366] Bowra, *Tradition and Design in the Iliad*: 62.
[367] Bowra, *Tradition and Design in the Iliad*: 62.
[368] Bowra, *Tradition and Design in the Iliad*: 63.
[369] Bowra, *Tradition and Design in the Iliad*: 63.
[370] Bowra, *Tradition and Design in the Iliad*: 63.
[371] Bowra, *Tradition and Design in the Iliad*: 63.
[372] Bowra, *Tradition and Design in the Iliad*: 64.

two main driving forces, simplicity and rapidity.[373]

In sum, Homer preserved some ancient devices of verse and decided what he could do with them. Further, he spent a lifetime perhaps perfecting his oral performances using an ancient oral tradition of Bronze Age Greece.

---

[373] Bowra, *Tradition and Design in the Iliad*: 66.

How does Homer employ the traditional epithet in his oral epics?

Homer's knowledge and imagination of a long tradition and use of diction is a key to his formulaic language. Milman Parry states, 'The epic poets fashioned and preserved over many generations a complex technique of formulae, a technique designed in its smallest details for the twofold purpose of expressing ideas appropriate to epic in a suitable manner, and of attenuating the difficulties of versification.[374] Bards found and kept expressions which could be used in a variety of sentences, either as they stood or with slight modifications, and which occupied fixed places in the hexameter line.[375]

These expressions are of different metrical length according to the ideas they are made to express; according to the nature of the words necessary for the expression of these ideas.[376] Of these formulae, the most common fill the space between the bucolic diaeresis[377] and the end of the line, between the penthemimeral caesura,[378] the caesura[379] *kata triton trohaion*, or the hephthemimeral caesura[380] and the end of the line, or between the beginning of the line and these, caesura; or else they fill an entire line.[381]

In sum, a study of Homer's epics and the different metrical lengths he employed is an insight into his genius in epic poetry to intensify the heroic stature of the subjects.

---

[374] Adam Parry ed., *The Making of Homeric Verse: The Collected Papers of Milman Parry*, Oxford, Clarendon Press, 1971: 9.
[375] Parry, *The Making of Homeric Verse*: 9.
[376] Parry, *The Making of Homeric Verse*: 9.
[377] Bucolic diaresis: a diaeresis after the fourth foot in a dactylic hexameter especially common in pastoral poetry. URL: https://www.merriam-webster.com/dictionary/bucolic%20caesura. Last Modified 25/8/2018.
[378] penthemimeral caesura: a caesura in classical verse occurring after the fifth half foot. URL: https://www.merriam- webster.com/dictionary/penthemimeral%20caesura. Last Modified 25/8/2018.
[379] caesura: a break in the flow of sound in a verse caused by the ending of a word within a foot. URL: https://www.merriam-webster.com/dictionary/caesura
[380] hephthemimeral caesura: a caesura in classical verse occurring after the seventh half foot. URL: https://www.merriam-webster.com/dictionary/hephthemimeral%20caesura. Last Modified 25/8/2018.
[381] Parry, *The Making of Homeric Verse*: 9.

What stock phrases did Homer use in describing the Gods? How did Pythagoras define the hidden measure behind all things which throws light on ancient Greek beliefs as reflected in Homer's epics? Was the stringed lyre player a forerunner of Homer's Singer of Tales from 1295 to 700 B.C.E.? How did music theory arrive in Greece during the Mycenaean Age 1600-1150 BCE? Was Greek music mainly enharmonic before Aristoxenus in the 4th century BC?

William Jones states that according the Aristoxenus: musicians ascribe to Olympus … the invention of enharmonic melody, and conjecture, that when he was playing diatonically on his flute, …from the highest of four sounds to the lowest but one, or … overlapping over the second in descent, or the third in accent, of that series, he conceived a singular beauty of expression; which induced him to dispose the whole series of seven or eight sounds by similar skips, and to frame by the same analogy the Dorian mode, omitting every sound peculiar to the diatonic and chromatic melodies … but without adding any that have since been made essential to a new enharmonic; in this genus, … he composed the Nome, or strain and Spondean,[382] because it was used in temples at the time of religious libations.[383] Interestingly, William James states that:

This method … of adding to the character and effect of a mode by diminishing the number of its primitive sounds introduced by a Greek of the lower Asia [Asia Minor], who flourished according to the learned and accurate writer of the *Travels of Anacharsis*, about [1250 BCE].[384] This means that bards or singer of tales or great poets in the courts of Mycenaean Kings had a far more advanced knowledge of music than previously thought. This is corroborated by archaeologist Anne Draffkorn Kilmer who comments on the *Tablet from Sippar circa 1800 BCE* in the context of music theory and the Sumerian and Akkadian nine stringed lyre.[385] She states, 'Fourteen distinct intervals are now recognized on the basis of this text:

---

[382] Spondee: a metrical foot consisting of two long or stressed syllables. URL: https://www.merriam-webster.com/dictionary/spondee. Last Modified 24/8/2018.

[383] William Jones, On The Musical Modes of the Hindus, 1781, 1799, pp.413-44. *Asiatic Researches 3*. URL: www.masseiana.org/jones4htm. Accessed 23 May 2016.

[384] Jones, "On The Musical Modes of the Hindus".

[385] Anne Draffkorn Kilmer, A Music Tablet from Sippar(?): BM 65217 + 6661, , *Iraq*. Vol. 46. No. 2 (Autumn, 1984), pp. 69-80 in British Institute for the Study of Iraq, URL: http://www.jstor.org/stable/4200216. Accessed 11-05-2016.

seven primary intervals of fifths and fourths, and seven secondary thirds and sixths'.[386]

Further, in the context of the tuning of the Babylonian harp 1500 BCE[387], as a precursor of the Greek lyre, David Wulstan states:

We now know that the Babylonians had seven octave species similar to but far antedating, those known from Greek sources. How far these theoretical, rather than practical, tunings we cannot at present tell. Nor can it be said on the basis of the material available so far, what connection, if any, the tunings had with modality if such a concept existed. The indications are, that Greek musical thought owed some debt to the Babylonians.[388]

In sum, it is possible that Mycenaean Kingdoms 1600-1150 BCE had gifted bards or singer of tales, who performed perhaps to a richer musical atmosphere than previously thought.

---

[386] Kilmer, "A Musical Tablet from Sippar".

[387] Bo Lawergren, *Ancient Harps*, URL: http://www.oxfordmusiconline.comezp.lib.unimelb.edu.au/subscriber/article/grove/music/45738/pg2?/ Babylonian Harp.

[388] David Wulstan, The Tuning of the Babylonian Harp in *Iraq*. Vol. 30. No. 2 (Autumn, 1968), pp. 215-228, British Institute for the Study of Iraq. URL: http://www.jstor.org/stable/4199852. Accessed 11-05-2016.

Aristoxenus, who taught music theory under Aristotle at the Lyceum, Athens,[389] stressed the importance of ear training.[390] He states, 'whether vocal or instrumental, our method rests in the last resort on an appeal to the two faculties of hearing and intellect.[391] By the former we judge the magnitudes of the intervals, by the latter we contemplate the functions of the notes.[392] The contrast between the Pythagorean and Aristoxenian views of musical science comes out strongly in the definitions of a tone.[393] For the Pythagoreans a tone is the difference between two sounds whose ratios of vibration stand in the relation 8:9; for the school of Aristoxenus, the difference between a Fourth and a Fifth.[394] The latter explains the phenomena of music by reducing these to more immediately known musical phenomena, the former by reducing them to their mathematical antecedents.[395]

Homer called the Okeanos [sky] the origin of gods and men.[396] The blend of imaginative, emotional and intellectual vigor which characterized the sixth and fifth centuries BCE in Greece; echoes the most abstract notions of the Boundless itself, which Anaximander describes as eternal and ageless, words which serve as a stock phrase in Homer to characterize the gods.[397] In the context of music theory and early Greek philosophy, Pythagoras argued that a hidden attunement governs the universe.[398] Pythagoras made a remarkable rediscovery in relation to the lyre. Measuring the lengths on the string of the lyre between the places where the four principal notes of the Greek scale were sounded, he found that they had the proportion 6:8:12.[399] This harmonic proportion contains the octave 12:6, the fifth 12:8, and the fourth 8:6.[400] Henri Frankfort indicates that it correlates musical harmonies, which belong to the world of the spirit no less than to that of sensual

---

[389] Annie Belis, *Aristoxenus*, URL: http://www.oxfordmusiconline.com.ezp.lib.unimelb.edu.au/ Accessed 17/5/2016.
[390] Henry Stewart Macran ed. trans., *The Harmonics of Aristoxenus*, New York: Georg Olms Verlag, 1974: 189.
[391] Macran, *The Harmonics of Aristoxenus*: 189.
[392] Macran, *The Harmonics of Aristoxenus*: 189.
[393] Macran, *The Harmonics of Aristoxenus*: 245.
[394] Macran, *The Harmonics of Aristoxenus*: 245.
[395] Macran, *The Harmonics of Aristoxenus*: 245.
[396] Henri Fankfort, H.A. Frankfort, John A. Wilson, Thorkild Jacobsen, and William A. Irwin, *The Intellectual Adventure of Ancient Man: An Essay on Speculative Thought in the Ancient Near East*, Chicago, The University of Chicago Press, 1977: 378.
[397] H. Frankfort, *The Intellectual Adventure of Ancient Man*: 380.
[398] H. Frankfort, *The Intellectual Adventure of Ancient Man*: 383.
[399] H. Frankfort, *The Intellectual Adventure of Ancient Man*: 383.
[400] H. Frankfort, *The Intellectual Adventure of Ancient Man*: 383.

perception, with the precise abstractions of numerical ratios.[401]

What constitutes the Homeric Formulae and Homeric Meter?

In general, Homer sought to avoid hiatus as something harmful to the rhythm of his verse.[402] I believe Homer had to remember the words, the expressions, the sentences he had heard from other bards who had taught him the traditional style of heroic poetry.[403] Further, he had to remember the innumerable devices which enabled him to combine these words and expressions into complete sentences and lines of six dactylic feet embodying the ideas proper to the narration of the deeds of heroes.[404] A Greek tradition and language, from generation to generation had preserved words and phrases which, could be drawn on for the making of poetry.[405]

Homeric bards are pursuing a twofold purpose of easy versification and heroic style; they had created a formulary diction and a technique for its use; provided the bard with materials of versification, which took on the shape of traditional things.[406] The proof lies in the sheer quantity of points of resemblance between the styles of the different parts of the poem.[407] Meaning, an accumulation of identical details of diction, whereby we see the poet or poets of the two poems making use of the same epithets and the same noun epithet formulae and reacting in the same way to the influence of the meter.[408]

---

[401] H. Frankfort, *The Intellectual Adventure of Ancient Man*: 384.
[402] Parry ed., *The Making of Homeric Verse:* 192.
[403] Parry, *The Making of Homeric Verse:* 195.
[404] Parry, *The Making of Homeric Verse:* 195.
[405] Parry, *The Making of Homeric Verse:* 195.
[406] Parry, *The Making of Homeric Verse:* 195.
[407] Parry, *The Making of Homeric Verse:* 189.
[408] Parry, *The Making of Homeric Verse:* 189.

How successful is Milman Parry's test in relation to Oral Traditions?

Milman Parry recorded the great Yugoslav bard Avdo Medjedovic, who performed seven long, epic verse narratives with a prodigious combined total of 41,818 decsyllabic[409] verses.[410] The shortest of these was 2,624 verses in length, while the longest came to 13,331 verses.[411] Albert Lord throws more light on Homer's style of composition by stating:

> The length of the Homeric poems, however, may well be due to the role of writing in their creation at the moment, or during the hours and days when Homer dictated them to a scribe. It is very likely, I believe, that Homer never sang the songs of the return of Odysseus from Troy or of the wrath of Achilles at the great length in which they appear in our *Iliad* and *Odyssey*.
> Like the *Kalevala* they were special poems in their composition. But the manner of composition of the Homeric poems was far different from that of the *Kalevala*. Homer was a bona fide traditional singer who had sung many songs many times in a tradition of singers like himself and songs like his. He expanded two of the songs in his normal repertory, when he dictated them. He did not stitch songs together to make his "monumental" songs, but he composed them in the manner of a living tradition such as those of the Slavs, which on occasion "mix" songs in order to create other, often carefully unified, songs. This is a different process, and one that has not yet been adequately described, from that of Lönnrot in compiling the *Kalevala*. The Homeric poems, on the contrary, were composed, I believe, in dictation in the same way in which Avdo Međedović's *The Wedding of Smailagić Meho* was composed in dictation.[412]

---

[409] decasyllabic: consisting of 10 syllables or composed of verses of 10 syllables. URL: https://www.merriam-webster.com/dictionary/decasyllabic. Last Modified 24/8/2018.

[410] David E. Bynum, *The Daemon in the Wood: A Study of Oral Narrative Patterns*, Cambridge, Harvard University Press, 1978: 297.

[411] Bynum, *The Daemon in the Wood*: 297.

[412] "The *Kalevala*, the South Slavic Epics, and Homer," by Albert Lord, Harvard University, URL: https://chs.harvard.edu/CHS/article/display/6183.6-the-kalevala-the-south-slavic-epics-and-homer. Last Modified 24/8/2018.

In sum, this provides us with a window into the oral epic tradition of Homer and the process of oral composition and practice, using stock epithets and using the speed of the lyre and bow to narrate his epic.

Examples of whole formulaic verses in Greek?

Homer's system of formulas involved two measures, that of length and that of thrift.[413] The length of a system consists very obviously in the number of formulas which make it up.[414] However, the most striking case in Homer is the system of noun epithet formulas for gods and heroes, in the nominative.[415] All the main characters of the *Iliad* and *Odyssey*, if their names can be fitted into the last half of the verse along with an epithet, have a noun epithet formula in the nominative, beginning with a simple consonant, which fills the verse between the trochaic caesura[416] of the third foot and the verse end; for example, Much devising Odysseus.[417] Homer's number of repetitions in a style, and the frequency with which they are used, bear directly upon the thrift of the diction.[418] I wish to point out, that this only provides an impression of the framework, which Homer used in his twenty- five or six thousand repetitions, of his 27853 or so verses.[419]

An example from the Homeric poems throws light in his style of composition in performance. In recounting the speeches in the assemblies of men or of gods in the *Iliad* Homer has several ways of noting the reactions of the assembly to a speech that has just been made. In three cases he reports that the men shouted, and in several instances the words of the speaker were met with silence. After he has indicated the reaction, Homer has a line leading to another speech. Two of the three shouting passages begin with the same couplet, and vary only in the third line, which introduces the next speaker. Here is the couplet:

Ὣς ἔφαθ', οἱ δ' ἄρα πάντες ἐπίαχον υἷες Ἀχαιῶν,
μῦθον ἀγασσάμενοι Διομήδεος ἱπποδάμοιο.

---

[413] Parry, *The Daemon in the Wood*: 276.
[414] Parry, *The Daemon in the Wood*: 276.
[415] Parry, *The Daemon in the Wood*: 276.
[416] Trochaic caesura: a metrical foot consisting of one long syllable followed by one short syllable or of one stressed syllable followed by one unstressed syllable. URL: https://www.merriam-webster.com/dictionary/trochees. Last Modified 24/8/2018.
[417] Parry, *The Daemon in the Wood*: 277.
[418] Parry, *The Daemon in the Wood*: 279.
[419] Parry, *The Daemon in the Wood*: 279.

So he spoke, and all the sons of the Achaians shouted acclaim, the word of Diomedes, breaker of horses.[420]

The third shouting passage differs from this couplet in its first and second lines:

Ὣς ἔφατ', Ἀργεῖοι δὲ μέγ' ἴαχον, ἀμφὶ δὲ νῆες σμερδαλέον κονάβησαν ἀϋσάντων ὑπ' Ἀχαιῶν,

So he spoke, and the Argives shouted aloud, and about them the ships echoed terribly to the roaring Achaians.[421]

The third and fourth lines of the preceding passage are:

μῦθον ἐπαινήσαντες Ὀδυσσῆος θείοιο.
τοῖσι δὲ καὶ μετέειπε Γερήνιος ἱππότα Νέστωρ·

as they cried out applause to the word of god-like Odysseus. Now among them spoke the Gerenian horseman, Nestor.[422]

Note that these two lines are variants of the second and third lines of the other two passages:

μῦθον ἀγασσάμενοι Διομήδεος ἱπποδάμοιο.
καὶ τότ' ἄρ' Ἰδαῖον προσέφη κρείων Ἀγαμέμνων.
τοῖσι δ' ἀνιστάμενος μετεφώνεεν ἱππότα Νέστωρ·

---

[420] "The *Kalevala*, the South Slavic Epics, and Homer," by Albert Lord, Harvard University, URL: https://chs.harvard.edu/CHS/article/display/6183.6-the-kalevala-the-south-slavic-epics-and-homer. Last Modified 24/8/2018.

[421] "The *Kalevala*, the South Slavic Epics, and Homer," by Albert Lord, Harvard University, URL: https://chs.harvard.edu/CHS/article/display/6183.6-the-kalevala-the-south-slavic-epics-and-homer. Last Modified 24/8/2018.

[422] "The *Kalevala*, the South Slavic Epics, and Homer," by Albert Lord, Harvard University, URL: https://chs.harvard.edu/CHS/article/display/6183.6-the-kalevala-the-south-slavic-epics-and-homer. Last Modified 24/8/2018.

the word of Diomedes, breaker of horses.[423]
and now powerful Agamemnon spoke to Idaios:
and now Nestor the horseman stood forth among them and spoke to them.[424]

When the reaction to a speech is silence, the passages (there are five of them) bridging that speech to the next begin with the line:

Ὣς ἔφαθ', οἱ δ' ἄρα πάντες ἀκὴν ἐγένοντο σιωπῇ,

So he spoke, and all of them stayed stricken to silence.[425]

Four of the passages end with a line introducing another speech by the same speaker. In three of them the speaker is Diomedes, and the line is the same:

ὀψὲ δὲ δὴ μετέειπε βοὴν ἀγαθὸς Διομήδης·

but now at long last Diomedes of the great war cry addressed them.[426]

In the fourth the speaker is Athena, and the line is varied to accommodate her name:

ὀψὲ δὲ δὴ μετέειπε θεὰ γλαυκῶπις Ἀθήνη·

But now at long last the goddess grey-eyed Athene answered him.[427]

---

[423] "The *Kalevala*, the South Slavic Epics, and Homer," by Albert Lord, Harvard University, URL: https://chs.harvard.edu/CHS/article/display/6183.6-the-kalevala-the-south-slavic-epics-and-homer. Last Modified 24/8/2018.

[424] "The *Kalevala*, the South Slavic Epics, and Homer," by Albert Lord, Harvard University, URL: https://chs.harvard.edu/CHS/article/display/6183.6-the-kalevala-the-south-slavic-epics-and-homer. Last Modified 24/8/2018.

[425] "The *Kalevala*, the South Slavic Epics, and Homer," by Albert Lord, Harvard University, URL: https://chs.harvard.edu/CHS/article/display/6183.6-the-kalevala-the-south-slavic-epics-and-homer. Last Modified 24/8/2018.

[426] "The *Kalevala*, the South Slavic Epics, and Homer," by Albert Lord, Harvard University, URL: https://chs.harvard.edu/CHS/article/display/6183.6-the-kalevala-the-south-slavic-epics-and-homer. Last Modified 24/8/2018.

[427] "The *Kalevala*, the South Slavic Epics, and Homer," by Albert Lord, Harvard University, URL: https://chs.harvard.edu/CHS/article/display/6183.6-the-kalevala-the-south-slavic-epics-and-homer. Last Modified 24/8/2018.

In the fifth case, although the next speaker is Diomedes, he is not resuming after the preceding speech, and the line is slightly different. It is like *Iliad* 2.336 in the shouting passages, except for the change of speakers:

τοῖσι δὲ καὶ μετέειπε βοὴν ἀγαθὸς Διομήδης·

but now Diomedes of the great war cry spoke forth among them.[428]

In two cases there are only two lines in the passage, and they have already been discussed. In the remaining three cases there are one or two lines of varying content between the beginning and the ending lines. It is to be noted, however, that the intervening lines have relatives in the other passages, both those with shouting and those with silence. Here, in their entirety, are the three cases in question:

Ὣς ἔφαθ', οἱ δ' ἄρα πάντες ἀκὴν ἐγένοντο σιωπῇ,
μῦθον ἀγασσάμενοι μάλα γὰρ κρατερῶς ἀγόρευσεν.
ὀψὲ δὲ δὴ μετέειπε θεὰ γλαυκῶπις Ἀθήνη·

So he spoke, and all of them, stayed stricken to silence, at his word, for indeed he had spoken to them very strongly. But now at long last the goddess grey-eyed Athene answered him.[429]

Ὣς ἔφαθ', οἱ δ' ἄρα πάντες ἀκὴν ἐγένοντο σιωπῇ,
δὴν δ' ἄνεῳ ἦσαν τετιηότες υἷες Ἀχαιῶν·
ὀψὲ δὲ δὴ μετέειπε βοὴν ἀγαθὸς Διομήδης·

So he spoke, and all of them stayed stricken to silence. For some time the sons of the Achaians said nothing, in sorrow;

---

[428] "The *Kalevala*, the South Slavic Epics, and Homer," by Albert Lord, Harvard University, URL: https://chs.harvard.edu/CHS/article/display/6183.6-the-kalevala-the-south-slavic-epics-and-homer. Last Modified 24/8/2018.

[429] "The *Kalevala*, the South Slavic Epics, and Homer," by Albert Lord, Harvard University, URL: https://chs.harvard.edu/CHS/article/display/6183.6-the-kalevala-the-south-slavic-epics-and-homer. Last Modified 24/8/2018.

but at long last Diomedes of the great war cry addressed them.[430]

Ὣς ἔφαθ', οἱ δ' ἄρα πάντες ἀκὴν ἐγένοντο σιωπῇ,
μῦθον ἀγασσάμενοι· μάλα γὰρ κρατερῶς ἀγόρευσε.
δὴν δ' ἄνεῳ ἦσαν τετιηότες υἷες Ἀχαιῶν·
ὀψὲ δὲ δὴ μετέειπε βοὴν ἀγαθὸς Διομήδης·

So he spoke, and all of them stayed stricken to silence at his words. He had spoken to them very strongly. For a long time the sons of the Achaians said nothing, in sorrow, but at long last Diomedes of the great war cry spoke to them.[431]

Albert Lord positively asserts that:
> The study of these passages indicates clearly that Homer, like the Finnish and
> South Slavic traditional poets in the passages from them analysed earlier, had
> in his mind a more or less stable unit of composition, with some lines very stable
> but others flexible enough to fit the contexts in which his narrative expressed itself.[432]

---

[430] "The *Kalevala*, the South Slavic Epics, and Homer," by Albert Lord, Harvard University, URL: https://chs.harvard.edu/CHS/article/display/6183.6-the-kalevala-the-south-slavic-epics-and-homer. Last Modified 24/8/2018.

[431] "The *Kalevala*, the South Slavic Epics, and Homer," by Albert Lord, Harvard University, URL: https://chs.harvard.edu/CHS/article/display/6183.6-the-kalevala-the-south-slavic-epics-and-homer. Last Modified 24/8/2018.

[432] "The *Kalevala*, the South Slavic Epics, and Homer," by Albert Lord, Harvard University, URL: https://chs.harvard.edu/CHS/article/display/6183.6-the-kalevala-the-south-slavic-epics-and-homer. Last Modified 24/8/2018.

What is the distinctive character of enjambement[433] in Homeric Verse? In relation to the Homeric sentence, Matthew Arnold states, 'he is eminently plain and direct, both in his syntax and in his words'.[434]

M. Maurice Croiset is closer to the mark, in stating, 'Complicated groupings of ideas are ... unknown, to Homeric poetry .... The ordinary law of this naïve and clear style is juxtaposition'.[435] What examples are found of Homer's Epic Technique of Oral Verse Making? Dionysius of Halicarnassus on *Literary Composition*, states, 'the clauses are not made like one another in form or sound, and are not enslaved to a strict sequence, but are noble, brilliant, and free'.[436] Meaning, ideas are added on to one another, in what Aristotle calls 'the running style'.[437]

In sum, Homer's style is reflective of a long tradition of oral verse making. Meaning a tradition of singing and performance which reflects how a bard or poet may have performed and sang epics at the court of Mycenaean Nobles 2700 years ago. Homer's timeless epics the *Iliad* and *The Odyssey* contain universal truths about human nature, society and religion. Historical records do not reveal the whole truth. The Song endures and is transmitted across 2700 years of recorded Greek history.

---

[433] Enjambement: the running over of a sentence from one verse or couplet into another so that closely related words fall in different lines. URL: https://www.merriam-webster.com/dictionary/enjambement. Last Modified 24/8/2018.
[434] Parry, *The Daemon in the Wood*: 251.
[435] Parry, *The Daemon in the Wood*: 251.
[436] Parry, *The Daemon in the Wood*: 252.
[437] Parry, *The Daemon in the Wood*: 252.

Is the Homeric language the language of an Oral Poetry? Homer uses enjambement in the *Iliad* and *Odyssey* about every fifth or sixth line, which is about twice as often as in the *Argonautica* or the *Aeneid*.[438]

Homeric language is the language of an oral poetry. For example, a group of six sentence verses to be found only in Homer *Iliad*.[439] What role did mimesis play in Homer's epics in the context of identity and poetic performance? How different is Homer's epics as fixed texts in contrast to shifting words in performance? Gregory Nagy points to five stages in the evolution and eventual crystallization of Homer's epics. For instance, the most fluid period with no written texts from 2000 BCE to 800 BCE; a Pan-Hellenic period with no written texts from 750 BCE to 650 BCE; a centralized Homeric performance based on potential texts in Athens; a standardizing period of texts during the reforms of Demetrius of Phalerum 317 to 307 BCE; finally, with a most rigid period with texts as scripture, with the completion of Aristarchus's editorial work on the Homeric texts.[440]

---

[438] Parry, *The Daemon in the Wood*: 255.
[439] Parry, *The Daemon in the Wood*: 255.
[440] Gregory Nagy, *Poetry as Performance: Homer and Beyond*, Cambridge, Cambridge University Press, 1996: 110.

Conclusion.

In sum, Homer, the improvisatory singer of tales, who reworked his cycle of ancient Greek tradition on the spot, in performance from mimesis has crystallized into written texts. A tradition introduced to Greek children for 2700 years. I was asked by my Greek school teacher, Ms. Alexandra, to memorize a page of Homer in primary school. I remember telling my father about the challenge of memorizing Homer's epics. My father reminded me of a huge tree, in the middle of the forest, of Lower Olympus, Thessaly, Greece. My father told me to visualize the huge tree; how all five members of the family could not join hands around the massive tree. To utilize the tree trunk as the Greek language; formed over 4000 years of tradition. How all the branches of the tree can be used to measure each sentence; each idea; each catalogue; each banquet; each battle scene.

To visualize looking up the tree trunk towards the sky. To place the Olympian Gods on top; to learn whom the gods favor and who they despise. To learn the character of each main protagonist. I practiced the scene of Achilles sulking in his tent; after the overbearing King Agamemnon had taken Briseis. Achilles makes the King realize just how much he needs him; as plagues bring devastation on the Greek army. And finally, the rage of Achilles, as he sets his sights on the destruction of Troy and is immortalized when Paris's arrow finds its mark. Daily singing and improvisation coupled with a long Greek tradition and a mastery of imagery and sounds and of the Greek language, is the key to understanding Homer and his epics.

Annotated Bibliography

Allen, Thomas W. *The Homeric Catalogue of Ships*, 1921.

Thomas W. Allen's *The Homeric Catalogue of Ships* sheds light on an original catalogue now lost on the Greek and Trojans who fought in the historical Trojan War circa 1125 BCE. The text of the Catalogue of Ships is in Attic Greek. It is divided into the following sections. An introduction; literature; other catalogues; ancient authorities; the Homeric Catalogue; The Greece of the Catalogue and Order of Places in the Catalogue. Chapter 1 relates to Central Greece. Chapter 2 relates to the Peloponnesus. Chapter 3 relates to North-West Greece. Chapter 4 relates to the Aegean Sea islands. Chapter 5 relates to North-Eastern Greece. Chapter 6 relates to the Trojan Catalogue and a conclusion. Chapter 7 relates to Nations Round Ida. Chapter 8 relates to European Allies. Chapter 9 relates to Asiatic Allies on the North Coast. Chapter 10 relates to Asiatic Allies on the West Coast. Chapter 11 relates to the author's conclusions. An appendix and maps are included.[441]

Ahrensdorf, Peter J. *Homer on the Gods & Human Virtue*, 2014.

Peter J. Ahrensdorf *Homer on the Gods & Human Virtue* examines Homer's understanding of the best life, the nature of the divine, and the nature of human excellence. Ahrensdorf argues that Homer teaches that human greatness eclipses that of the gods. Pointing out that the contemplative and compassionate singer ultimately surpass the heroic warrior in grandeur; and that it is the courageously questioning Achilles, not the loyal Hector or even the wily Odysseus, who comes closest to the humane wisdom of Homer himself. He argues that Homer's triumph is shedding light on two distinctive features of Greek civilization. It's extraordinary celebration of human excellence, as can be seen in Greek athletics, sculpture, and nudity, and its singular questioning of the divine, as can be seen in Greek philosophy.[442]

Albracht, Franz. *Battle and Battle Description in Homer*, 2005.

---

[441] Thomas W. Allen, *The Homeric Catalogue of Ships*, Oxford: Clarendon Press, 1921: ix – xi.
[442] Peter J. Ahrensdorf, *Homer on the Gods & Human Virtue*, Cambridge: Cambridge University Press, 2014: 251.

Franz Albracht's *Battle and Battle Description in Homer* examines the state of military practice as depicted in the heroic age of Homer's Mycenean Greece. Part I begins with an introduction to Homer's descriptive battle scenes and the principles characters. It then covers the Council of War. Marshalling of the Army throughout the Mycenean Kingdoms of Greece. Use of Chariots. Advance into Battle. The Standing Fight. Massed Attack and the Defense to it. Retreat, Flight and Pursuit followed by notes. Part II begins with an introduction. Protection Against the Enemy. Attack on and Defense of a Fortified Camp. Siege and Defense of a Fortified City. With notes. In addition, it contains a bibliography, index and appendix by Malcolm Willcock.[443]

Bowra, C. W. *Tradition and Design in the Iliad*, 1930.

The author sees that there is a problem and is willing to discuss it. His position, indicated already in the title, seeks to avoid extremes and is described (p. 1) as excluding "on the one hand. . . . the view that the completed poem is largely the result of chance and caprice,' and on the other hand the view that the poet was completely his own master and the Iliad is what it is simply because Homer chose so to compose it." The topics treated may be suggested by a quotation of the chapter head- ings: "Tradition and Design" (pp. 1-26); "The Origins of the Epic" (pp. 27- 52); "The Hexameter" (pp. 53-66); "Some Primitive Elements" (pp. 67-86); "Repetitions and Contradictions" (pp. 87-113); "The Similes" (pp. 114-28); "The Language" (pp. 129-55); "The Historical Background" (pp. 156-91); "The Characters" (pp. 192-214); "Homeric Theology" (pp. 215-33); "Homer and the Heroic Age" (pp. 234-50); "Homer's Time and Place" (pp. 251-78). The author's strength lies in his literary appreciations, and these constitute the best and the largest portions of the book. "It is now possible," he says (p. 1), "to take the Iliad as we have it and to consider it as poetry".[444]

Chadwick, John. *The Decipherment of Linear B*, 1958, 1990.

---

[443] Franz Albracht, *Battle and Battle Description in Homer*, London: Duckworth & Co, 2005.
[444] C. W. Bowra, *Tradition and Design in the Iliad*, Oxford: The Clarendon Press, 1930.

John Chadwick's account of Michael Ventris's decipherment of Linear B which revealed an early form of Greek from the late Helladic period 1300 BC is rich in technical detail and demonstrates the early form of Greek. Figures provide a straight forward methodology of how Michael Ventris discovered that Linear B is an archaic form of Greek. This account includes: A Chart of eighty- seven signs, with numerical equivalents and phonetic values. 1. Mycenaean sites and places mentioned on the Linear B tablets. 2. Greek dialects about 400 B. C. 3. Heiroglyphic tablet from Phaistos. 4. Linear A Tablet from Hagia Triada. 5. The development of cuneiform script. 6. The Cypriot syllabary. 7. Comparison of signs in Linear B and classical Cypriot. 8. Kober's triplets. 9. Pylos Tablet Aa62 showing composition of text. 10. Some obvious ideograms. 11. Sex differentiation of the ideogram PIG. 12. The building of the grid. 13. Ventris' grid, 28 September 1951. 14. A Knossos chariot table. 15. A Knossos sword tablet. 16. Mycenaean vessels and their names.[445] Chadwick convincingly argues' that the Linear B tablets and Homer's epics the *Iliad* and the *Odyssey* are a song sung by the last and greatest bards. A long line of poets from 1600 – 1100 BCE sung about the time when Mycenaean Kingdoms were organized into a strong centralized network of kingdoms. The influence of this network of Mycenaean Kingdoms were felt throughout the Mediterranean, Anatolia and the Middle East. Homer is not a historian, but one of the world's great poets.

Chadwick, John. *The Mycenaean World*, 1976.

John Chadwick who assisted Ventris in the decipherment of Linear B an archaic form of Greek summarizes the latest findings which open a window to the world of the Mycenaean Greeks. Despite the clay tablets only being the accounts of anonymous clerks. What can be gleaned from them is a bronze industry, foreign slave women, and even human sacrifice.[446] Chadwick begins by listing all illustrations. Eleven chapters follow: 1. The Hellenization of Greece. 2. The Documentary evidence. 3. Mycenaean geography. 4. The people of the tablets. 5. The social structure and the administrative system. 6. Religion. 7. Agriculture. 8. Craft, industry and trade. 9. Weapons and war. 10. Homer the pseudo-historian. 11.

---

[445] John Chadwich, *The Decipherment of Linear B,* Cambridge: Cambridge University Press, 1958: Preface.
[446] John Chadwick, *The Mycenaean World*, Cambridge: Cambridge University Press, 1976: Preface.

The end of the Mycenaean world. A Bibliography and Index complete this remarkable work.[447]

Clay, Jenny Strauss. *Homer's Trojan Theatre*, 2011.

Moving away from the verbal and thematic repetitions that have dominated Homeric studies and exploiting the insights of cognitive psychology, this highly innovative and accessible study focuses on the visual poetics of the Iliad as the narrative is envisioned by the poet and rendered visible. It does so through a close analysis of the often-neglected 'Battle Books'. They here emerge as a coherently visualized narrative sequence rather than as a random series of combats, and this approach reveals, for instance, the significance of Sarpedon's attack on the Achaean Wall and Patroclus' path to destruction. In addition, Professor Strauss Clay suggests new ways of approaching ancient narratives: not only with one's ear, but also with one's eyes. She further argues that the loci system of mnemonics, usually attributed to Simonides, is already fully exploited by the Iliad poet to keep track of his cast of characters and to organize his narrative. Provides a detailed analysis of the Iliad's landscape that embraces Troy, the Greek camp, and above all the battlefield. Shows how visual memory and mnemonics allow the poet of the Iliad not only to keep track of his large cast of characters, but also to keep his narrative on track. Outlines how an ancient text and modern cognitive psychology can mutually illuminate each other.[448]

Foley, John Miles. *The Theory of Oral Composition*, 1988.

Foley focusses on the development of the Oral Formulaic Theory from its origins in the writings of Milman Parry and Albert Lord through its contemporary influence on more than one hundred language traditions. He starts with a brief exploration of contributions to the fields of philology, anthropology, and the debate on the Homeric question in classical studies that formed a direct or indirect influence of Parry. The succeeding chapters focus on field work in 1934 and 1935.

---
[447] Chadwick, *The Mycenaean World*: Contents.
[448] Jenny Strauss Clay, *Homer's Trojan Theatre*, Cambridge: Cambridge University Press, 2011: Preface.

The fourth chapter The Making of a Discipline summarizes the application of the theory of oral composition devised by Parry and Lord to a select number of traditions, ancient Greek, Old English, Serbo-Croatian, Hispanic, Old French, medieval German, Byzantine and modern Greek, Irish, biblical studies, Arabic, African and more. The final chapter points out significant recent contributions to the debate and Foley concludes with brief suggestions for future directions.[449]

Friedrich, Rainer. Formular Economy in Homer, 2007.

Rainer Friedrich's *Formular Economy in Homer* is in two parts which examine orality in Homer's epics, the *Iliad* and the Odyssey. 1. Formular Economy in Homer. Observance and Breach. 1. Introduction. The Four Tests of Orality. 2. The Principle of Formular Economy. a. Economy and Schematization. b. What is, and What is not, a Breach of Economy? c. Formular Economy and Reduced Extension. d. Metrical Equivalence and Semantic Difference. e. The Argument from Thrift: Main Plank of the Theory of the Oral Homer. 3. The Breaches of Formular Economy in *Iliad* and Odyssey. a. Prelude to the Economy Test. b. The Name epithet Systems for Achilleus and Zeus. a. Tables 1 and II. c. The Evidence for Breaches of Economy in *Iliad* and Odyssey. a. General Considerations on the Evidence. b. A Note on Method. g. Table III. A General List of Breaches of Economy. d. Formular Economy in Homer: A Preliminary Conclusion.[450]

Part II. The Poetics of the Breaches. 1. Introduction. Three Avenues to the Poetics of Breaches. 2. Deliberate Variatio. a. Variatio in Oral Composition and Iteratio in Phrase Clusters. b. Case studies of Deliberate Variato. c. A List of Further Instances of Deliberate Variatio. 3. The Avoidance of Stylistic Infelicities and Contextual Unsuitability. 4. Escaping the System. The Pursuit of Justness of Expression. a. A Critical Recapitulation of Parryist Reasoning on the Epithet. b. Breach of Economy and Stylistic justesse in Particularized Formulas. c. The phrase juste in Homer. Case Studies. 5. Beyond Schematization. a. Oblique Expressions. b. The Stylistic Effect of Oblique Expressions. Some Cases in Point. 6.

---

[449] John Miles Foley, *The Theory of Oral Composition,* Bloomington: Indiana University Press, 1988.
[450] Rainer Freidrich, *Formular Economy in Homer: The Poetics of the Breaches*, Stuttgart: Franz Steiner Verlag, 2007: 5-6.

Conclusion. Towards Schema free Composition. a. The Relaxation of Formular Economy and Schematization. b. Parryism's Dilemma and its Possible Resolution. Followed by a bibliography, indices, index rerum and index locorum.[451]

Hainsworth, J. B. *The Flexibility of the Homeric Formula*, 1968.

J. B. Hainsworth's *The Flexibility of the Homeric Formula* provides key insights into Homer's method of improvisation in relation to oral performance and orality. For instance, Homer begins in the tenth and final year of the Trojan War and narrates the Catalogue of Ships, the Royal Families of Greeks and Trojans and detailed descriptions of battle scenes rich in imagination and with some kernel of historical significance. The Contents contain the following chapters. 1. Composition with Formulae. 2. Personal Name Formulae: Some Irregularities. 3. What is a Formula? 4. Mobile Formulae. 5. Modification. 6. The Expansion of Formulae. 7. Separation. 8. The Flexible Formula. Followed by Tables and an Index. The Tables provide a rare insight into the improvisational art of Homer and his use of nouns in an expressive context with a juxtaposed attributive epithet whether decorative or functional. It conveys a vivid picture of how the bard or bards may have performed at Mycenean Kingdoms in Greece between 1400 BC to 1100 BC.[452]

Hoeckstra, A. Epic Verse before Homer, 1981.

The argumentation of the book could be presented as follows: the evidence we have, is that the oldest formulae for different reasons (of both form and content) must be of Mycenaean date, and that they exactly fit the formulaic systems we know; and as these systems exactly fit the hexameter, it follows that these systems and the hexameter must be of Mycenaean date. And "after the scattered remnants of the old population had gained a stable foothold on the foreign coasts (of Ionia) and had settled down to more or less peaceful conditions, the memories of a splendid and distant past led to a revival of the mainland epic." Here I would ask

---

[451] Friedrich, *Formular Economy in Homer*, 2007: 5-6.
[452] J. B. Hainsworth, *The Flexibility of the Homeric Formula*, Oxford: Clarendon Press, 1968.

whether perhaps our definition of formula does imply that it fits the hexameter. So perhaps we disregard old elements that do not fit, as being problematic. I don't think so, but it may be good to formulate the question. The conclusion is, I think, that we have to show how probable it is that certain elements are of Mycenaean date. This study adduces more evidence, but primarily sketches the conclusions to be drawn from them. It becomes time for something like a systematic commentary on the (oldest) formulae, bringing together the evidence in a handbook. (In this book one misses an index of the words and formulae studied).[453]

Hunter, Richard. *The Measure of Homer: The Ancient Reception of the Iliad and the Odyssey*, 2018.

Richard Hunter's, *The Measure of Homer* argues that Homer was the greatest and most influential Greek poet. He explores central themes in the poem's reception in antiquity, paying attention to Homer's importance in shaping ancient culture. Subjects include the geographical and educational breadth of Homeric reception, the literary and theological influence of Homer's depiction of the gods. Homeric poetry and rhetorical approaches to Homer are also covered. He explores how Homer is depicted in the satires of Plutarch and Lucian and how Homer shaped ideas about the power of music and song. He also provides translations of Homer in Greek and Latin.[454]

Kirk, G. S. *Homer and the Epic*, 1965.

Kirk's vivid and comprehensive account of the background and development of the Homeric poems and of their quality as literature. His purpose remains the same: to develop a comprehensive and unified view of the nature of the Iliad and the Odyssey, of their relation to the oral heroic poetry of the Greek Dark Age, and of their creation as poems by two great singers in the eighth century BC. The essential attitudes and arguments of the earlier work have been retained, but the whole has

---

[453] Beekes, R. S. P. *Mnemosyne*, Fourth Series, 37, no. 1/2 (1984): 161-65. http://www.jstor.org.ezp.lib.unimelb.edu.au/stable/4431314.
[454] Richard Hunter, *The Measure of Homer: The Ancient Reception of the Iliad and the Odyssey*, Cambridge: Cambridge University Press, 2018.

been reduced in detail by some two-fifths. The sections on the historical background, the possibilities of Achaean and Aeolic epic, and the technical aspects of the language have been abbreviated most, and those dealing with oral poetry and the Iliad and Odyssey as literature least of all. Professor Kirk has also changed the order and increased the number of chapters. Almost all the Greek is translated, and the new version can be more easily used by those who are primarily interested in classics in translation, comparative literature, oral poetry, or the epic in general.[455]

Lord, Alfred. *The Singer of Tales*, 2000.

This 40th anniversary edition of Albert Lord's classic work includes a unique enhancement: a CD containing the original audio recordings of all the passages of heroic songs quoted in the book; a video publication of the kinescopic filming of the most valued of the singers; and selected photographs taken during Milman Parry's collecting trips in the Balkans.

Parry began recording and studying a live tradition of oral narrative poetry in order to find an answer to the age-old Homeric Question: How had the author of the *Iliad* and *Odyssey* composed these two monumental epic poems at the very start of Europe's literary tradition? Parry's, and with him Lord's, enduring contribution--set forth in Lord's *The Singer of Tales*--was to demonstrate the process by which oral poets compose.
Now reissued with a new Introduction and an invaluable audio and visual record, this widely influential book is newly enriched to better serve everyone interested in the art and craft of oral literature.[456]

Jensen, Minna Skafte *The Homeric Question and The Oral Formulaic Theory*, 1980.

Minna Skafte Jensen's *The Homeric Question and The Oral Formulaic Theory* contains the following chapters. Chapter 1. An Introduction. Chapter 2. The Frame of Reference; The selection of material; Which literary forms are comparable?

---

[455] G. S. Kirk, *Homer and the Epic*, Cambridge: Cambridge University Press, 1965: Preface.
[456] Alfred B. Lord, *The Singer of Tales,* London: Harvard University Press, 2000: Preface.

How valid is the oral theory? Chapter 3. Quality as an Argument against Orality; The IIiad and the Odyssey compared to the Epic Cycle; Compositional patterns in the IIiad and Premeditation and correction. Chapter 4. Quality as an Argument against Orality; Large scale epics orally composed; The sociology of epic in the IIiad and the Odyssey; The sociology of ancient Greek epic; Length of the IIiad and the Odyssey. Chapter 5. Poetics as an Argument for Orality; Poetics of Serbian oral epic singers; Theory and practice; Descriptions of singers in the IIiad and the Odyssey; Information on the poet's own ambitions; Hesiodic poetics and a Conclusion. Chapter 6. The IIiad and the Odyssey as Oral Dictated Texts; Lord's three degrees of oral composition; The process of dictation; The transitional text and the initiative for the recording in writing. Chapter 7. The Writing of the IIiad and the Odyssey in Sixth Century Athens; The terminus post quem; The terminus ante quem and the History of the Vulgate. Chapter 8. Oral Composition in the Sixth Century; Creativity and reproduction on oral tradition; The Singers in the Odyssey; The rhapsodes and When was oral composition, brought to an end in Greece? Chapter 9. The Pisistratean Recension. Arguments pro et contra. The evidence. Plutarch's theory. References to Homer in political disputes. Interpolations. Homer brought to the mainland. The institution of rhapsodic recitals at the Panathenaea. The collecting of Homer's poems. Chapter 10. The IIiad, the Odyssey, and the Cultural Policy of Pisistratus. The cultural policy of Pisistratus. Oral epic as a conveyor of ideology. Marks of Pisistratus Athens in the IIiad and the Odyssey. It also contains a section on Notes, Bibliography, Ancient Passages Discussed, General Index, Appendix: Sources Referred to in Chapter IX and a Table of the Evidence Discussed in Chapter IX.[457]

Morris, Ian and Powell, Barry. *A New Companion to Homer*, 1997.

This volume is the first English-language survey of Homeric studies to appear for more than a generation, and the first such work to attempt to cover all fields comprehensively. Thirty leading scholars from Europe and America provide short, authoritative overviews of the state of knowledge and current controversies in the many specialist divisions in Homeric studies. The chapters pay equal attention to

---

[457] Minna Skafte Jensen, *The Homeric Question and The Oral Formulaic Theory*, Copenhagen: Museum Tusculanum Press, 1980: Contents.

literary, mythological, linguistic, historical, and archaeological topics, ranging from such long-established problems as the "Homeric Question" to newer issues like the relevance of narratology and computer-assisted quantification. The collection, the third publication in Brill's handbook series, *The Classical Tradition*, will be valuable at every level of study - from the general student of literature to the Homeric specialist seeking a general understanding of the latest developments across the whole range of Homeric scholarship.[458]

Nagy, Gregory. *Poetry as Performance: Homer and Beyond*, 1996.

Gregory Nagy's *Poetry as Performance: Homer and Beyond* examines performance and composition as the key drivers behind the bards who sang Homer's *Iliad* and Odyssey in Mycenean Kingdoms between 1400 and 1100 BC. The contents of the book are in the following sections. Introduction: a brief survey of concepts and aims. Part I: Mimesis and the making of identity in poetic performance. 1. The Homeric nightingale and the poetics of variation in the art of a troubadour. 2. Mimesis, models of singers, and the meaning of a Homeric epithet. 3. Mimesis of Homer and beyond. 4. Mimesis in lyric: Sappho's Aphrodite and the Changing Woman of the Apache. Part II: Fixed text in theory, shifting words in performance. 5. Multiform epic and Aristarchus' quest for the real Homer. 6. Homer as script. 7. Homer as scripture. Epilogue: dead poets and recomposed performers. Appendix. Bibliography and an Index.[459]

Page, Denys. *History and the Homeric Iliad*, Berkeley, University of California Press, 1972.

Denys Page's *History and the Homeric Iliad* is an important addition to Homeric studies. Page points out that the Odyssey has plot and structure which can reveal something of the process followed by Homer or the long line of poets in the selection of verses that they originally sung in Mycenaean Courts. Page assesses the historical status of the Trojan War and considers the extent to which, or how knowledge of that encounter descended to the composer of the *Iliad*. The strength

---

[458] Ian Morris & Barry Powell, *A New Companion to Homer*, Leiden; New York: Brill, 1997. Preface.
[459] Gregory Nagy, *Poetry as Performance: Homer and Beyond*, Cambridge: Cambridge University Press, 1996: vii.

of this work is the mention of the Mycenean Greeks known as Achaeans in Hittite Documents in the first chapter. Chapter 2: The History of Troy. 3. The Historical Background of the Trojan War. 4. The Homeric Description of Mycenaean Greece. 5. The Documents from Pylos and Cnossos. Chapter 6. Some Mycenaean Relics in the Iliad. Appendix: Multiple Authorship in the Iliad. I. The Embassy of Achilles. II. The Achaean Wall. And an Index.[460]

Parry, Adam. *The Making of Homeric Verse: The Collected Papers of Milman Parry*, 1971.

Adam Parry's *The Making of Homeric Verse*, examines the key elements of the Homeric Formula from the *Iliad* and Odyssey. The Contents provides a List of Abbreviations and an Introduction. 1. The Traditional Epithet in Homer. 2. Homeric Formulae and Homeric Metre. 3. The Homeric Gloss: A Study in Word sense. 4. The Distinctive Character of Enjambement in Homeric Verse. 5. Studies in the Epic Technique of Oral Verse Making I Homer and Homeric Style. 6. Studies in the Epic Technique of Oral Verse Making II. The Homeric Language as the Language of an Oral Poetry. 7. The Traditional Metaphor in Homer. 8. Whole Formulaic Verses in Greek and South-Slavic Heroic Song. 9. The Traces of the Digamma in Ionic and Lesbian Greek. 10. On Typical Scenes in Homer. 11. The Historical Method in Literary Criticism. 12. About Winged Words.[461]

II. Summaries of Unpublished Works. 13. The Homeric Metaphor as a Traditional Poetic Device. 14. Homer and Huso: I The Singer's Rests in Greek and South-Slavic Heroic Songs.[462]

III. Unpublished Works. 15. A Comparative Study of Diction as one of the Elements of Style in Early Greek Epic Poetry. 16. Cor Huso: A Study of South-Slavic Song. Extracts.[463]

IV. By A. B. Lord. 17. Homer, Parry, and Huso. Index of Names and Subjects.

---

[460] Denys Page, *History and the Homeric Iliad*, Berkeley, University of California Press, 1972: Contents.
[461] Adam Parry Editor. *The Making of Homeric Verse: The Collected Papers of Milman Parry*, Oxford: Clarendon Press, 1971. Contents.
[462] Parry, *The Making of Homeric Verse*, 1971. Contents.
[463] Parry, *The Making of Homeric Verse*, 1971. Contents.

List of Plates.[464]

Parry, Anne Amory *Blameless Aegisthus: A Study of Amymon and Other Homeric Epithets*, 1973.

Anne Amory Parry, Blameless Aegisthus: A Study of Amymon and Other Homeric Epithets focusses on Homeric vocabulary which illuminate for a modern audience early Greek concepts of body, soul, mind, thought, choice and so on. Parry's purpose in this book is to hit back at Homerists who malign Homer by saying that he uses adjectives in a very casual way and sometimes uses one in a context where it is inappropriate.[465] Parry bravely takes as the instrument of her attack the notorious phrase in the first book of the Odyssey where Zeus uses the word *amumon* to characterize the adulterer and murderer Aegisthus.[466] Parry argues convincingly that Homeric epithets are not ordinarily chosen for their special relevance to the immediate context. Since the great majority of epithets is honorific, and since Homeric heroes ordinarily are lauded, and not disparaged, the epithets are roughly interchangeable and can be selected according to metrical needs. Parry provides an insight into the mind of a bard of the caliber of Homer who chooses a noun epithet formula of the right length, no matter which epithet it contains. Parry points to how precise and subtle Homer used phrases and his incredible formulaic systems.

Rayor, Diane J. *The Homeric Hymns*, 2004.

Diane J. Rayor's, *The Homeric Hymns*, is a methodical and elegant approach to the Homeric Hymns which have captivated audiences for over 2,500 years. The Homeric Hymns is a collection of thirty-four poems: thirty- three invoke and celebrate the gods and one addresses hosts either the hosts of the immediate

---

[464] Parry, *The Making of Homeric Verse*, 1971. Contents.

[465] Frederick M. Combellack, " *Blameless Aegisthus: A Study of AMYMŌN and Other Homeric Epithets* . Anne Amory Parry ," Classical Philology 72, no. 2 (Apr., 1977): 167-173. https://doi.org/10.1086/366343

[466] Frederick M. Combellack, " *Blameless Aegisthus: A Study of AMYMŌN and Other Homeric Epithets* . Anne Amory Parry ," Classical Philology 72, no. 2 (Apr., 1977): 167-173. https://doi.org/10.1086/366343

performance or all those in general who provide hospitality. The Hymns are Homeric because they are composed in the same traditional epic meter or dactylic hexameter, dialect, and style as Homer's Iliad and Odyssey. They are hymns in that each poem celebrates the attributes or epiphany of the god or goddess to whom the hymn is addressed. The Hymns provide introduction to the principal ancient Greek deities, and they include some of the earliest literary references to key religious rituals and sites.[467]

In conclusion, the Homeric Hymns point to the religious life of Greeks in Homeric times. The Hymns celebrate a god. The Hymns end with a prayer to a god.

Richardson, Nicholas *The Iliad: A Commentary. Volume VI: Books 21-24*, 1993.

Nicholas Richardson's *The Iliad: A Commentary* begins with a Preface and an Abbreviations section. An introduction. Three chapters. 1. Structure and themes.

a) Structure. ii) Themes. 2. Two special problems. i) Book Division. ii) The end of the Iliad in relation to the Odyssey. 3. Homer and his ancient critics.

b) From Homer to Aristotle. ii) The Hellenistic period. iii) Rome to the Augustan period. iv) Later Greek criticism. v) Neoplatonists and Christians. Commentary divided into four parts: Book 21. Book 22. Book 23. Book 24. Followed by a General Index to Volume VI. Index of Greek words for all volumes pages 369-387.[468]

Sacks, Richard, *The Traditional Phrase in Homer*, 1987.

This study attempts to bridge the now classic gap between fixed form and functioning context which continues to limit our understanding of theHomeric phrase. The first part of the study uses the presence of Homeric phrases in other Greek poetry, especially the notoriously "Homeric" Theognis 237-254, to help identify potentially significant phrases. The second part considers the epithets of Hector, in an attempt to re-examine Parry's notion of traditional fixed epithets and their importance for understanding the *Iliad* and the *Odyssey*. The author offers original interpretations of the workings of the traditional

---

[467] Diane J. Rayor, *The Homeric Hymns*, Berkeley: University of California Press, 2004: Introduction.
[468] Nicholas Richardson, *The Iliad: A Commentary: Volume VI: Books 21-34*, Cambridge: Cambridge University Press, 1993: Contents page.

phrase in Homer, also of Theognis 237- 254 and of the *Iliad*'s much-debated characterization of Hector. Along the way, Sacks suggests how his method may help with other problems, including contested emendations in Homer, the relationship of the *Iliad* and the *Odyssey*, and the relationship between epic and other genres. The central concern of the book, however, is the traditional artistry of Homer.[469]

Benjamin Sammons, *The Art and Rhetoric of the Homeric Catalogue*, 2010.

Benjamin Sammons, work captures the idealization for an epic like the *Iliad* and Odyssey by the ancient bard known as Homer. Pietro Pucci puts it succinctly, stating: The catalogue, as a speech act, manifests a prowess of memory, and points to poetry as its privileged means. Cataloguing constitutes the supreme distillation of poetry's capabilities for truth, rigor, order, history, [in sequence]: mere names, mere numbers, and no metis, or as we would say no connotations, no rhetoric, no fiction. Almost no poem.[470] Richardson convincingly points out that the catalogue is an efficient device for the poet to accomplish a major task without complicating that

narrative.[471] For instance, catalogues of people help the poet to communicate the size of the Achaean army or its Trojan counterpart, which is a necessary step in his representation of the Trojan War as a conflict of huge armies, besides providing an opportunity to introduce or replenish his cast of characters.[472]

In conclusion, this work provides the poet with the means to convey a great performance in the Mycenaean Kingdoms between 1600-1100 BCE.

Sanders, N. K. *The Epic of Gilgamesh*, 1960.

Gilgamesh, King of Uruk, and his companion Enkidu are the only heroes to have survived from the ancient literature of Babylon, immortalized in this epic poem that dates back to the third millennium BC. Together they journey to the Spring of Youth, defeat the Bull of Heaven and slay the monster Humbaba. When Enkidu dies, Gilgamesh's grief and fear of death are such that they lead him to undertake a quest for eternal life. A timeless tale of morality, tragedy and pure adventure, *The Epic of Gilgamesh* is a landmark literary exploration of man's search for immortality. N. K. Sandars's lucid, accessible translation

---

[469] Richard Sacks, *The Traditional Phrase in Homer*, Leiden: E. J. Brill, 1987: Introduction.
[470] Nicholas Richardson, *The Iliad: A Commentary. Volume VI: Books 21-24,* Cambridge: Cambridge   University Press, 1993:19.
[471] Nicholas Richardson, *The Iliad: A Commentary. Volume VI: Books 21-24,* Cambridge: Cambridge   University Press, 1993:19.
[472] Nicholas Richardson, *The Iliad: A Commentary. Volume VI: Books 21-24,* Cambridge: Cambridge   University Press, 1993:19.

is prefaced by a detailed introduction that examines the narrative and historical context of the work. In addition, there is a glossary of names and a map of the Ancient Orient.[473]

Scott, William C. *The Artistry of the Homeric Simile*, 2009.

William C. Scott's *The Artistry of the Homeric Simile* are treasure troves. They describe scenes of Greek life that are not presented in their simplest form anywhere else: landscapes and seascapes, storms and clam weather, fighting among animals, civic disputes, athletic contests, horse races, community entertainment, women involved in their daily tasks, men running their farms and orchards. Scott argues that these paratactic additions to the narrative show how the Greeks found and developed parallels between two scenes – each of which elucidated and interpreted the other – then expressed those scenes in effective poetic language.[474] Scott explores the variations and modifications that Homer employs in order to make similes blend expressively with the larger context. In conclusion, he points to the richness of Homer.[475]

Stanley, Keith *The Shield of Homer: Narrative Structure in the Iliad*, 1993.

Keith Stanley's work begins with a list of illustrations. Followed by five chapters. 1. Form and Interpretation in Homer. 1. The Shield of Achilles as a Problem in Interpretation. 2. Ring Composition in Homeric Digressions. 3. The Function of Ring Composition in the Description of the Shield. 4. Structure and Interpretation in the Catalogue of Ships: Implications for the Shield. 5. Oral Theory and the Question of Structure. 6. Previous Views of Homeric Form. 7. The Organization of Narrative outside Digressions. II. The Structure of IIiad 1-7. III. The Structure of Iliad 8-17. IV. The Structure of Iliad 18-24. V. Structure and the Homeric Question. 1. Some Implications for the Nature of Our Iliad. 2. The Question of Book Division and Closure. 3. The Practical Function of the Book Groups. 4. Orality versus Literacy in the Iliad. 5. The Date and Context of Our Iliad. 6. Our Iliad and Homer's. Acknowledgments. A Note on Documentation and Usage. Notes. Bibliography and Index.[476]

Tsagarakis, Odysseus, *Nature and Background of Major Concepts of Divine Power in Homer*, 1977.

Odysseus Tsagarakis's work begins with a Preface. Introduction. Chapter 1. Zeus. a. Supreme in power. b. Supports man. c. Gives algae. d. Punishes wrongdoers. e. Co-operates

---

[473] N. K. Sanders, Translator, *The Epic of Gilgamesh*, Harmondsworth, Middlesex: Penguin Books, 1960: Preface.
[474] William C. Scott, *The Artistry of the Homeric Simile*, Lebanon: Dartmouth College Press, 2009: Back cover.
[475] William C. Scott, *The Artistry of the Homeric Simile*, Lebanon: Dartmouth College Press, 2009: Back cover.
[476] Keith Stanley, *The Shield of Homer: Narrative Structure in The Iliad*, Princeton: Princeton University Press, 1993: Contents page.

with other gods. Chapter 2. Apollo. a. Aids man. b. Harms man. Chapter 3. Athena. a. Helps man. b. Harms man. Chapter 4. Theoi or Gods. a. Fulfil wishes. b. Give olbos, time and character qualities. c. Protect and support. d. Gives algae. e. Punish the insolent. Chapter 5. Theos or God. a. Fulfils wishes. b. Makes gifts. c. Supports man. d. Gives kaka. algae and sorrows. e. Inspires man. Chapter 6. a. Aids man. b. Harmful intervention. c. Inspires. Chapter 7. Moira or Fate. a. Is powerful. b. Overcomes man. c. Associated with Zeus. Chapter 8. Conclusion. Select Bibliography. Indexes: I. Greek Index. II. General Index. III. Index passages.[477]

Tsagalis, Christos. *The Oral Palimpsest: Exploring Intertextuality in the Homeric Epics*, 2008.

Oral intertextuality is an innate feature of the web of myth, whose interrelated fabrics allow the audience of epic song to have access to an entire horizon of diverse variants of a story. *The Oral Palimpsest* argues that just as the erased text of a palimpsest still carries traces of its previous writing, so the Homeric tradition unfolds its awareness of alternative versions in the act of producing the signs of their erasure.[478]

In this light, "Homer" reflects the concerted effort to create a Panhellenic canon of epic song, through which we can still retrieve the poikilia (roughly, "dappled, embroidered variation") of various interwoven fabrics belonging to recognizable song-traditions or even older Indo-European strata.[479]

Woodhouse, W. J. *The Composition of Homer's Odyssey*, 1930.

Professor Woodhouse's analysis of the Odyssey goes far to establish the fact that a Saga of Odysseus actually existed. He also makes some exceedingly interesting conjectures as to its contents. He finds an important trace of its existence in the line of the Exordium of the Odyssey which refers to Odysseus as the man who had seen the cities of many men. Although the poem purports to contain a full account of the

---

[477] Odysseus Tsagarakis, *Nature and Background of Major Concepts of Divine Power in Homer*, Amsterdam: B. R. Gruner Publishing, 1977: Contents.
[478] Christos Tsagalis, *The Oral Palimpsest: Exploring Intertextuality in the Homeric Epics*, Washington D.C. Harvard University Press, 2008: Back cover.
　Christos Tsagalis, *The Oral Palimpsest: Exploring Intertextuality in the Homeric Epics*, Washington D.C. Harvard University Press, 2008: Back cover.

Wanderings, the promise implied in that line is not fulfilled. Professor Woodhouse concludes from this fact and from a consideration of a number of other passages in the poem that there was in existence at the time of the composition of the Odyssey a tradition which attributed to Odysseus adventures different from those described in the Odyssey and that the Exordium of the Odyssey originally constituted the exordium of the Saga in which that tradition was embodied. His theory is that the

Saga told the story of the adventures of Odysseus during the year or more following the fall of Troy and concluded with an account of his return to Ithaca and his suppression, with the aid of a few faithful retainers, of a revolutionary movement which had been launched by some would-be usurpers of his rule during his absence. Notwithstanding the author's conclusion that a Saga of Odysseus actually existed, it is a cardinal element of his view of the Odyssey that it is a romance based on the old story of the Returned Husband and in no sense a mere amplification of the historical or quasi-historical Saga.[480]

---

[480] W. J. Woodhouse, *The composition of Homer's Odyssey*, Oxford: The Clarendon Press, 1930: Preface.

Bibliography

1. Barnes, Jonathan. *Early Greek Philosophy*, London, Penguin Books, 1987.

2. Barnes, Jonathan. Ed. *The Complete Works of Aristotle* 2 volumes, Princeton, Princeton University Press, 1984.

3. Beckman, Gary M. Bryce, Trevor R. and Cline, Eric H. *The Ahhiyawa Texts*, Atlanta, Society of Biblical Literature Press, 2011.

4. Bowra, C. M. *Tradition and Design in the Iliad*, Oxford: Oxford University Press, 1963.

5. Bryce, Trevor. *Kingdom of the Hittites*, Oxford; New York; Oxford University Press, 2005.

6. David E. Bynum, David E. *The Daemon in the Wood: A Study of Oral Narrative Patterns*, Cambridge, Harvard University Press, 1978.

7. Chadwick, John. *The Decipherment of Linear B*, Cambridge, Cambridge University Press, 1958: 7.

8. Chadwick, John. *The Mycenaean World*, Cambridge, Cambridge University Press, 1991: 182.

9. Clay, Jenny Strauss. *Homer's Trojan Theater: Space, Vision, and Memory in the Iliad*, Cambridge, Cambridge University Press, 2011: 14.

10. Fagan, Brian M. *People of the Earth: An Introduction to World Prehistory*, Santa Barbara, Longman Press, 1998.
11. Fagles, Robert. Translator, *Homer: The Iliad*, New York: Penguin Group, 1990.
12. Fagles, Robert. Translator, *Homer: The Odyssey*, New York, Penguin Group, 1990.
13. Faulkner, R. O., translator, *The Ancient Egyptian Pyramid Texts*, Oxford: Oxford University Press, 1969.

14. Foley, John Miles. *The Theory of Oral Composition: History and Methodology*, Indianapolis, Indiana University Press, 1988.

15. Fankfort, Henri. Frankfort, H.A. Wilson, John A. Jacobsen, Thorkild. and William A. Irwin, William A. *The Intellectual Adventure of Ancient Man: An Essay on Speculative Thought in the Ancient Near East*, Chicago, The University of Chicago Press, 1977.

16. Georgiades, Thrasybulos, translated by Erwin Benedikt and Marie Louis Martinez, *Greek Music, Verse and Dance*, New York, Da Capo Press, 1955.

17. Hainsworth, J. B. *The Flexibility of the Homeric Formula*, Oxford, Clarendon Press, 1968.

18. King, Billie Jean. *The Hittites and their World*, Atlanta, Society of Biblical Literature, 2007.

19. Kirk, G. S. *Homer and The Epic: A Shortened Version of The Songs of Homer*, Cambridge, Cambridge University Press, 1976: 224.

20. Lord, Albert B. *The Singer of Tales*, Cambridge, Harvard University Press, 2000.

21. Ludwig, Emil. *Schliemann of Troy: The Story of a Gold-seeker*, London, Unwin Brothers Limited, 1931.

22. Macran, Henry Stewart, Ed. Trans. *The Harmonics of Aristoxenus*, New York: Georg Olms Verlag, 1974.

23. Melchart, Craig H. *Luwians*, Boston, Brill Academic Publishers, 2003.

24. Meyer, Karl E. *The Plundered Past: The Traffic in Art Treasures*, Trowbridge & Esher, Redwood Burn Limited, 1974.

25. Morris, Ian. Powell, Barry B. Ed. *A New Companion to Homer*, New York, E.J. Brill, 1997.

26. Nagy, Gregory. *Poetry as Performance: Homer and Beyond*, Cambridge, Cambridge University Press, 1996.

27. O'Brien, John Maxwell. *Alexander the Great: The Invisible Enemy*, London, Routledge Press, 1992.

28. Page, Denys L. *History and the Homeric Iliad*, Berkeley, University of California Press, 1966.

29. Parry, Adam. Ed., *The Making of Homeric Verse: The Collected Papers of Milman Parry*, Oxford, Clarendon Press, 1971.

30. Prasad, R. C. *Tulasidasa's Shriramacharitamanasa (The Holy Lake of the Acts of Rama)*, New Delhi, Motilal Banarsidass Publishers, 1990.

31. Parry, Anne Amory. *Amymon and Other Homeric Epithets*, Leiden, E. J. Brill Publishers, 1973.

32. Sandars, N. K. translator, *The Epic of Gilgamesh*, Harmondsworth, Penguin Books, 1972.

33. Scott, William C. *The Artistry of the Homeric Simile*, Lebanon, Dartmouth College Press, 2009:

34. Woodhouse, W. J. *The Composition of Homer's Odyssey*, Oxford: Clarendon Press, 1969.

Electronic Journals

Annie Belis, Aristoxenus, URL: http://www.oxfordmusiconline.com.ezp.lib.unimelb.edu.au/, Accessed 17/5/2016.

Annie Belis, Aulos, URL:http://www.oxfordmusiconline.com.ezp.lib.unimelb.edu.au/subscriber/article/grove/music /01532?q =Aulos, Accessed 29/4/2016.

Kilmer, Anne Draffkorn. A Music Tablet from Sippar(?): BM 65217 + 6661, , *Iraq.* Vol. 46. No. 2 (Autumn, 1984), pp. 69-80 in British Institute for the Study of Iraq, URL: http://www.jstor.org/stable/4200216. Accessed 11-05-2016.

Edwards, Mark W. Homer and Oral Tradition: The Formula, Part I in *Oral Tradition*, ½ (1986): 171-230. URL: http://www.journal.oraltradition.org/files/articles/1ii/2_edwards.php Accessed 22/5/2016.

Hainsworth, J.B. The Homeric Formula & The Problem of its Transmission, *Bulletin of the Institute of Classical Studies*, 9:57-68. doi: 10.1111/j.2041-5370.1962. tb00696.x

Huxley, G. L. Historical Criticism in Aristotle's "Homeric Questions", , *Proceedings of the Royal Irish Academy*. Section C: Archaeology, Linguistics, Literature, Vol. 79 (1979), pp.73-81. Published by: Royal Irish Academy, URL: http://www.jstor.org/stable/25506363. Accessed: 22/05/2016.

Jones, William. On The Musical Modes of the Hindus, 1781, 1799, , pp.413-44. *Asiatic Researches 3.* URL: www.masseiana.org/jones4htm. Accessed 23/5/2016.

Lawergren, Bo. Ancient Harps, , URL: http://www.oxfordmusiconline.comezp.lib.unimelb.edu.au/ subscriber/article/grove/music/45738/pg2?/ Babylonian Harp. Accessed 20/5/2016.

Joseph Russo. "A Closer Look at Homeric Formulas." *Transactions and Proceedings of the American Philological Association* 94 (1963): 235-47., URL: http://www.jstor.org/stable/283649 doi: 1.

Mass, Martha, *Phorminx* URL:http://www.oxfordmusiconline.com.ezp.lib.unimelb.edu.au/subscriber/article/grove/music /21597? Accessed 29/4/2016.

Sale, William Merritt. Homer and the Roland: The Shared Formula Technique, Part II, , in *Oral Tradition*, 8/2 (1993): 381-412. URL: http://www.journal.oraltradition.org/files/articles/8ii/7_sale_part Accessed 22/5/2016.

Sale, William Merritt. "The Trojans, Statistics and Milman Parry", , Greek, Roman and Byzantine Studies Library, last modified May 22, 2016. URL: http://www.grbs.library.duke.edu/article/download/4241/5559 page 341.

Wulstan, David. The Tuning of the Babylonian Harp in *Iraq*. Vol. 30. No. 2 (Autumn, 1968), pp. 215- 228, British Institute for the Study of Iraq. URL: http://www.jstor.org/stable/4199852. Accessed 11-05-2016.

DVD's
Ulysses, Directed by Mario Camerini, (Rome, Paramount Pictures, 1954). DVD.
Troy, Directed by Wolfgang Petersen, (Malta, Warner Bros. Pictures, 2004. DVD.

www.ingramcontent.com/pod-product-compliance
Lightning Source LLC
Chambersburg PA
CBHW080226170426
43192CB00015B/2762